Flight to Freedom

JEAN KLIER

Copyright © 2017 Jean Klier

All rights reserved.

ISBN:0995367620
ISBN-13: **978-0995367623**

To
Miriam and Lex Cullen
for their encouragement
to tell this story.

'Just living is not enough.
One must have sunshine, freedom
and a little flower.'

Hans Christian Andersen

JEAN KLIER

GLOSSARY OF PIDGIN WORDS AND PHRASES

p.9	meri	woman, women
	pikinini	baby, child
	pitpit	bamboo beaten and woven into matting
p.10	Yumi statem long nem bilong Papa Got, na Pikinini bilong em Jisas, na Holi Spirit.	
	= We begin in the name of Father God, his son Jesus and the Holy Spirit.	
	Jisas em i as bilong olgeta samting = Jesus is the foundation of everything	
p.11	Jisas em i bagarap olgeta, em I bagarap finis. Jisas im dai long diwai kras	
	= Jesus was altogether broken on a wooden cross, Jesus died on a wooden cross.	
p.15	masta	master
	mi lukim	I see
p.18	wantok's kar	car (literally one talk)
p.19	buai	betel nut
p.21	laplap	length of material wrapped round the waist like a skirt
p.23	yu laikim	do you like it? / would you like it?
p.27	mi go kisim dring	I will get a drink
	wara bilong kokonas	coconut water
p. 32	i kirap	gets going
	orait yumi go tumora	all right, we'll go tomorrow.
	singsing	dance with chanting
p.33	bilum	string bag used to carry anything from vegetables to babies
p.34	tapa	cloth made from tree bark
	pulpul	grass skirt
p.35	haus tambaran	spirit house
p. 36	kiap	government officer (from Australia at this time)
p.37	kunai	grass to make a roof
p. 38	haus sik	aid post, hospital
	polis	police
	dokta	doctor, first aider
	namasusu	soft drink

p. 40	stap plis	stop please
	mi laik tokim dispela man =	I want to talk to this man
	kaukau	sweet potato
p.46	em i orait	it's all right
p.47	mi no save toktok bilong em	I don't understand their language
p.52	sapos mi go isi isi trak i pas	if I go carefully the truck would get stuck
	sapos mi tokim yu olsem yu prêt no gut tru =	if I told you about it you would have been very frightened
	bel bilong mi i olsem kabis	my stomach feels like a cabbage
	rot i orait nau?	is the road all right now?
	em i orait liklik	it's all right a little bit, sort of
p.53	orait yo mekim kamap olsem	all right you make it happen
	sikispela man em inap	six men will be enough
	mipela laik go daun	we want to get down
p. 58	em i stap	he is here / is he here?
	asde em i go finis	yesterday he left for good
	bilong wanem?	why?
p.60	kaikai redi	food is ready
p.64	cuscus	a possum with golden fur
	as gras	leaves used to cover bottoms
p.72	olsem wanem?	what is this?
p.74	gutpela rot long Laiagam?	is it a good road to Laiagam?
	liklik	little
	bihain em i nogut tru	later it is really bad
	mi yet slip long kar	I will sleep on the truck
	nogut ol i stilim cargo	no good if they steal the cargo
	haus man	men's house
	kasen bilong mi i stap	this is my cousin
	yu laik kisim manki masta	do you want a house boy
	bipo em i wok long Surunki	he used to work at Surunki
	em i save tok Pisin?	Does he understand Pidgin
p.75	mi traim, em i gut or nogat	I will try him out to see if he is good or not
	mi painim Akali	I will find Akali
p.76	yumi wetim Roland, em i no kamap yet =	we will wait for Roland, he is not here yet
	yumi no slip long kar	we won't sleep in the truck
p.79	tenk yu	thank you
	barets	deep drains

FLIGHT TO FREEDOM

p.81 didiman — agricultural officer
p.87 lotu — church
p. 90 gutpela umu — a good hangi pit used to cook food in the ground (New Zealand)
    mumu — as above but called mumu in New Guinea
    yumi nogat bulmakau, bikpela kakaruk i stap, lukim = we don't have a cow, a big chicken is here, look
p.91 ol i kukim long graun mipela kolim mumu = when we cook in the ground we call it mumu
    long ples bilong me ol i kolim umu = where I come from we call it umu
p.103 yu go kwiktaim long rot — go quickly on the road
    mekim kar i go hariap — make the truck go fast
p.104 mekim i go bek isi isi — go back slowly, carefully
    yu stap long hia — you stay here
    oraitim bris sapos you ken — fix the bridge if you can
    na wetim mi — then wait for me
p.111 bung (pron. boong) — a get together
p.119 yu mekim wanem long hia? — what are you doing here?
    raus! nau! — go! now!
    yu mekim nogut tru! — you are doing something really bad!
    yu kam long wanem lain? — what tribe do you belong to?
    sapos yu kam bek, mi singautim polis. = if you come back I will call the police.
p.136 moningtaim raunwara i stap long arasait = in the morning the lake is on the other side
p.137 apinun i go bek, raunwars i stap hia = in the afternoon it goes back and stays here
p.145 yumi mekim wanem? — what will we do?
    skus mi masta — excuse me master
p.151 Mi laikim planti. Hau mas? — I would like plenty. How much are they?
p.197 Isi, isi! Holim! Holim pas! Paslm! = Carefully! Hold it! Hold it fast! Fasten it!

JEAN KLIER

CHAPTER ONE

Dieter slept most of the night and dreamed about his future. The train ground on and in the morning they arrived in Sydney. There Dieter went to the People's Palace and booked in. He requested that they wake him at seven o'clock the next morning and ordered a taxi for 7.45 a.m. to go to the airport. The rest of the day he strolled around King's Cross in the vicinity of the People's Palace. He was careful to keep the grey stone building in his sight so that he would not get lost. In the evening he ordered a meal of fish and chips at a cafe followed by a cup of tea and biscuits. It was such a novelty to be free to control his life, alone in a comfortable way.

At Kingsford Smith airport the next morning Dieter looked around in amazement. The entrance hall was brightly lit with a tiger moth now silent and motionless suspended from the ceiling. All around him people were immaculately dressed for travel, chattering excitedly or saying tearful goodbyes. Dieter approached one of the airport staff and asked for directions. Once he had checked in his luggage he wandered over to the tall plate glass windows and watched the air traffic. Planes whined as the props began to whirl and reached a crescendo. The window where Dieter stood vibrated as the blades became a blur and each plane in turn taxied out for takeoff.

At length his flight was called and the passengers were ushered out onto the tarmac and along a roped path, some to the front and Dieter's group to the rear of an imposing T-jet. It was long and sleek compared to some of the other aircraft he had been observing. Silver grey undercarriage, a blue line containing the row of windows with white on top and the TAA insignia. The pungent smell of refuelling invaded his nostrils. At the top of the steps in the belly of the plane stood two smiling stewardesses dressed in smart grey costumes with matching pillbox hats perched at a jaunty angle on their heads. Dieter showed his boarding pass like those in front had done.

"On the right six rows down, by the window Sir," she said.

"Thank you." Dieter nodded and smiled. He was pleased that he had a window seat. With a whine the jet engines announced their presence one at a time and they soon taxied out to the runway. Dieter marvelled at the immense power as he was pushed back into his seat and held there while the plane sped down the runway and soared steeply up through the clouds.

As the plane circled and headed north Dieter watched Sydney disappear from view. In no time at all lunch was served by the cabin crew – small helpings of delectable food all served in individual containers on a folding tray lowered from the seat in front. Dieter had never travelled by plane before so he took his cue from the man next to him. Most of the time he was reading a newspaper and Dieter was amazed at his dexterity in such a confined space. After lunch Dieter settled back to gaze at the clouds around him and dream. He was sure he must be very close to heaven. Whether he slept or not he was not certain, when he came to with a start.

"As we are now approaching Port Moresby please return to your seats and fasten your seat belts," a stewardess intoned over the speaker system. Once Dieter had complied with the instructions he sat forward and watched as his capsule took him into a different time zone. The coast far below them was rocky with palm trees dotting the shore. Thatched houses on stilts stood in the water. Further inland the vegetation was sparse and not so lush. His ears crackled and popped like the rice bubble advertisement as they descended into Moresby. Dieter held his nose and forced air into his ear canals to try and clear them.

"Welcome to Port Moresby. Please ensure you take all your belongings with you as you leave this craft. Thank you for travelling with TAA."

Approaching the rear door dressed in his winter Sunday best the heat slammed into Dieter. It felt as though someone had left on all the heaters. On the way to the terminal he divested himself of a gaberdine overcoat and then his sports jacket. Still he was sweltering!

As he waited for his suitcase he loosened his tie, undid his top button, took off his jumper and rolled up his shirtsleeves. That was better but still stifling. Wangaratta could be hot in summer but he did not remember it being like this. He was in the tropics.

It turned out there were three single men including Dieter and they were all in the same boat, dressed for winter. They began chatting as they moved across to check in for the flight to Lae. This is where they would be working for Namasu, a supply arm of the Lutheran Mission in New Guinea.

Lae fitted Dieter's dream of a tropical paradise more than Port Moresby. Here the grey sands of the beach were lined with palms that seemed to nod in approval. People dotted the beaches with bright clothing and fishing boats sailed on a sea of serenity. Dr Fugmann was waiting at the airport.

"Welcome," he said as he shook each young man's hand. "Please come." With luggage and excess clothing in hand they followed him out to a beige Mercedes. "I'll take you to your accommodation first to leave your belongings. Then we'll go to my home where Mrs Fugmann is preparing a meal."

"Thank you." The young men all answered. Food sounded good!

At the single men's quarters at Voco Point they chose their rooms, left their suitcases and returned to the Mercedes.

It was getting towards dusk as they drove up. The Fugmann's home had a corrugated iron roof, with woven pitpit walls that extended 3 feet up from the floor on two sides of the dining area. Above that there were louvre windows and fly screen wire to keep out the insects. A cool breeze fanned their faces as the new arrivals took in the ambience of the place. A large native wood table was set with care as the house girls bustled about putting the finishing touches to the meal under Mrs Fugmann's guidance. Their new boss led them into the sitting room. Here, while he smoked his pipe, they were all served freshly pressed fruit juice.

The meal consisted of a variety of delicious salads and chicken. Afterwards they were served coffee.

"Grown in our own compound and roasted on site," Mrs Fugmann said as she wafted the steam towards her with a hand. "Delicious!"

"Roy will take you home," Mr Fugmann put in. Obviously it was time to depart. "In the morning is church. I will see you there." No questions asked, it was expected.

After farewells and thanks to the Fugmanns they were ushered out to Roy's truck. Roy jumped into the driver's seat and Dieter climbed in the passenger's side while Dick and Ian sat on the back. Roy stuck his head out the window.

"Want to have a beer on the way home? At the Melanesian. It's just new and the only pub in town."

"Why not?" They all agreed.

"This is the life," Dick said as they leaned on the bar with a 4X beer in front of them and a cigarette.

"Sure is," Dieter added.

Later back at their quarters they all said good night and Dieter for one was glad to go to bed. It had been a long and eventful day.

"Thank you God for showing me the path to freedom," he said as he drifted off to sleep.

CHAPTER TWO

Dieter woke in the morning to new sounds and a new environment. He had arrived but he still had trouble believing it. His bedroom was upstairs – a closed in veranda overlooking the Huon Gulf with black volcanic sand on the beach. He could see the end of the airstrip. Tall palms in front of the window swayed and rustled in the breeze. Two fishing boats approached the beach with their early morning catch.

After breakfast Dieter looked through his meagre wardrobe for the coolest clothes. Mrs Fugmann was right – they would need to go shopping tomorrow for clothing suitable for the tropics. Then they all piled into the truck and headed for church. The sun shone and the day was warming up already. Swarms of native people were heading in the same direction. The church bell heralded that church would begin soon. As they parked the truck Dieter could see the triangular wooden frame housing the bell that was calling them to divine worship. The church, an imposing sight with a concrete floor, appeared to hover a foot above the ground. Woven pitpit wall panels at shoulder height surrounded the building. Steel posts grounded it and supported the corrugated iron roof. The Fugmanns waited near the door greeting people they knew. Colourful clothing and smiling faces were highlighted against the crisp cream house of worship. Man, meri and pikinini flocked in. As the new arrivals approached Mr Fugmann stepped forward and welcomed them.

"Would you like to sit with us," he said to Dieter.

An air of reverence pervaded the atmosphere inside as they quietly took their pews. There were spaces between the wall panels where folk could enter or exit the building with a cream ceiling overhead. At the front of the church wooden steps climbed to the sanctuary, where the altar stood on a polished wooden dais.. Two brass candlesticks stood at each end of the white cloth, flickering gently as the breeze wafted through. A simple brass cross stood in the centre behind an open Bible. Dieter wondered what language was written there. It did not really matter he supposed. It was a symbol of holy God communicating with mere mortals in whatever language. Behind the altar a large wooden cross was silhouetted against a painted wall.

The air was fresh. Dieter could smell frangipanis on the breeze mingled with soap and talcum powder on the expectant faithful. The church had been well designed to suit the climate. A hush descended as a door opened and two clergy emerged, their white cassocks contrasted against their dark skins. The younger gentleman was short and stocky with greying hair. The other, aged with white hair, was tall and imposing. Both wore green stoles and carried themselves with dignity as they moved to take up their positions. Pastor Zurewe (the younger) walked to the front of the platform while Bishop Kuder (the taller) took up one of two seats along the wall. Not that Dieter knew their names at this time. Later he came to know them and respect them.

The service was in pidgin Dieter realised with a start.
"Yumi statem long nem bilong Papa Got, na Pikinini bilong em Jisas, na Holi Spirit," Pastor Zurewe intoned.
The voices rose in a hymn of praise of God and escaped the church through the upper opening to wend the chorus heavenward. Dieter was familiar with the well-known tune but the words were foreign to him. After prayer, a congregational confession and another hymn Bishop Kuder rose up in the lectern and towered even higher over them all. He prayed a blessing in pidgin then read from the Scripture. His texts came from Krais i Kamapim Tok long Jon o Revelesen (Revelations) and Wok bilong ol Aposel (Acts of the Apostles) not that Dieter understood that either. But he listened or attempted to see if he could understand some of it. He was awed by this new experience in a different culture. Things began to unravel for Dieter when the Bishop announced in a strong voice, "Jisas emi as (pronounced arse) bilong olgeta samting."

Dieter was shocked and glanced at Mr Fugmann to read his reaction. He looked straight ahead and did not even flinch. Not wanting to make a scene Dieter settled down and listened again. Maybe he should not have! The second barrage to his religious senses was as bad as the first and followed quickly on its tail.

"Jisas im dai long diwai kros. Jisas em i olgeta bagarap, em i bagarap finis!"

At this point Dieter went red in the face. He could contain himself no longer and must leave this place of sacrilegious blasphemy. As he tried to stand up Dr Fugmann pressed a hand strongly on his knee, preventing him from doing so.

"I'll explain later," he whispered.

Dieter glanced around him. No one else seemed perturbed. A young baby suckled contentedly under his mother's blouse. An old man coughed. All the adults listened with rapt attention, some nodding in agreement.

After a final hymn and a blessing the ordeal was over. Mr Fugmann led the way out past Bishop Kuder as he shook hands with the parishioners. Bishop Kuder beamed at the young men and wished them well for their time in Lae. Dieter felt relief as he left the precinct and they followed the Fugmanns home to share Sunday dinner. Mrs Fugmann and the house girls bustled around with final preparations while her husband talked to the young fellows.

"Church is in pidgin, a language derived from a mixture of four others – Malay, German, English and Portuguese," he explained.

"But wouldn't it be easier to learn the tribal language. This sounds too complicated for me," Dick put in.

"Well the problem is there are so many different languages in New Guinea. Over 200 in fact and some tribes haven't been discovered yet. They are still counting. So we have a real mixture here of people from many tribes," Mr Fugmann went on.

"Why not English then? Why make up a new language?" Dick was not convinced.

"Why not German? Why not Kâte? I'll tell you why not! Pidgin is relatively easy to learn."

"Didn't sound too good to me in the sermon. The Bishop was swearing I thought," Dieter said.

"It might sound like it. Bagarap is useful in many instances – for a truck breakdown, if anything breaks in fact. So 'Jisas emi bagarap finis' simply means he was killed, completely broken. As for 'as' it means the foundation, the beginning."

"Didn't sound like that," Dieter said with a grin.

"No but you all need to learn pidgin," Fugmann concluded.

CHAPTER THREE

It was a warm balmy evening as the boys set out in the truck for Bumayong High School. They had been invited by the girls – teachers – who lived in the nearby hostel. Dieter admired the vibrant colours and inhaled tropical scents as they sped along the white coral road. Neat hedges of hibiscus surrounded the Europeans' houses. Frangipani trees spread their branches to share a heavenly perfume. Bromeliads lined the road in the shade of taller vegetation. Tree ferns dotted the rainforest as they wound along the valley. Finding purchase in the trees sprays of orchids lent their colours alongside trailing vines of bouganvillea.

At length they pulled up outside the teachers' hostel. A light was on at the door and geckos lurked on the walls, chattering to each other, waiting for a tasty morsel to fly by. Perfumed gingers stood in a clump nearby.
"Welcome one and all," Marie said as she answered the door gong.
The girls certainly had made their accommodation attractive. Frangipani flowers floated in a glass bowl on the table. A hoya plant draped itself up and over a white painted dresser, the pink flowers hanging like bells. The table was set and the aroma coming from the kitchen told the boys that dinner was well on the way. Whirring quietly above their heads the ceiling fan blended everything together. Over a meal of sweet and sour fish on rice, they got to know each other, talking about their work in Lae and what they had been doing before they came to the Territory. Dieter talked about his work at the mills and his involvement with youth group and church. No one

seemed to notice that he did not mention his family and no one asked any questions. It was good to discuss their first impressions and have a laugh about pidgin and their attempts to learn it.

"We manage don't we boys," Dick said.

"What we don't know we make up."

"Yes," added Dieter, "and we can always act it out too."

"As long as you keep it decent," Roy joked.

"Well, I certainly didn't think much of the Bishop Kuder's language at our first church service. It seemed anything goes, until Fugmann explained it to us," Dieter said.

The girls laughed. Of course the girls taught classes in English. The pupils came from outlying villages where they had attended a mission primary school. Only the top scholars were able to gain a place in high school.

"What about some coffee and cake!" suggested Jane.

"Good idea!" they all agreed.

A tropical downpour hammering the tin roof over their heads made conversation difficult. But it didn't matter while they ate dessert and drank coffee. It would cease as quickly as it started.

"Your turn to come to us next time," Roy said as they thanked the girls for a scrumptious meal and enjoyable evening.

"Sure," they replied, "let us know when."

"Will do," they said as they walked out to the truck.

Dieter noticed the musty, earthy smell after the rain. Marauding flying foxes screeched in the fruit trees looking for their supper. Bananas, mangoes, papaya– anything would do. They drove back along the road with the windows down listening to the calls of the night birds – owls and nightjars. Coming round a bend they were startled as a sudden jolt went through the vehicle.

"Ah, that hurt," Roy yelled shaking his hands.

"What happened?"

"Hit a bloody python," he explained. "Must have been a biggy, really jarred my hands."

"Does it happen often?" Dieter asked.

"Na, after rain you have to be careful. That's when they are most likely to slide out of the trees. It seems they can't hang on when it's slippery."

"So do you just leave it there for some other poor bugger?" Ian asked.

"No it'll be gone by now. Good tucker as far as the villagers are concerned."
"You're having us on!" Ian said.
"No fair dinkum!"
"Have you eaten snake? What does it taste like?"
"Never," Roy replied. "I haven't been that desperate."

CHAPTER FOUR

Dieter enjoyed life in his tropical paradise but he also worked. After all Namasu had paid his airfare to New Guinea to facilitate that. As far as Dieter was concerned it felt like one long holiday compared to two shifts a day in Wangaratta. Now he was in charge of his own finances with his mother so far away. Letters still came from time to time but they did not shout at him or hit him round the ears and he could choose if and when he read them.

Namasu was a supply base for the Lutheran missionaries in the outposts. Dr Fugmann had set it up as a subsidiary of the Lutheran mission. Initially it was housed in a Quonset hut. He had called it Namasu meaning the kernel of the coconut, the food which had sustained the native people for generations, known as the tree of one thousand uses. The work day started at 8 am through to 12 noon. Then it was a stroll home for lunch prepared by the house boy, followed by a siesta till 2 o'clock. Work finished at 5 in the evening. He was paid $56 per week after all board and food money had been deducted. Dieter's job was to manage the bulk store. The merchandising manager ordered goods from overseas and Darrel attended to the transfer of the cargo from the docks to the warehouse.

"Here's the truck," Dieter called to Toby and Mambu.
"Yes Masta, mi lukim," Toby replied as the Abco truck, a surplus army vehicle, pulled in to inward goods where two huge doors stood open. The driver handed Dieter the bill of lading so that he could

check items as Toby and Mambu unloaded everything and put them into the designated bays.

The warehouse had been built in a u-shape around the two storey office block. On either side of the office were outward goods and inward goods. The bulk store was kept cool and airy with a high ceiling the height of two floors of offices. Along the back wall were stairs leading to a mezzanine floor where lighter goods such as clothing, kitchen utensils, enamel plates and cups, cutlery, tools and cashboxes were kept. Large heavy items were stored on the ground floor, bags of rice, sugar and salt, cartons of mackerel, MaLing chicken and duck, bully beef, sao crackers, marie biscuits and cabin bread. Round the outside of the building louvre windows and open doors kept the building ventilated. The wooden exterior was coated with creosote, a contrast to the white window frames. Fly wire covered the windows and kept out the insects.

Once the truck was unloaded Dieter and his team began to fill orders for trade stores on the outlying stations. An order on a clipboard was attached to a trolley and off they went. A bay was designated for each outpost where the order was checked, ready for delivery. Huge Oshkosh trucks backed up to the outward goods section to ingest orders and transport them for eight hours or longer up the Markham Valley to the Kassam Pass and onto Kainantu and Goroka via the Daulo Pass, stocking all Namasu bases as they went.

For the afternoon siesta Dieter lay on his bed under the fan dreaming of his future. Today there had been a letter from home waiting for him and it needed his attention. It had been written at Mutti's request by a neighbour. A begging letter. Your mother cannot pay the electricity bill because the children need school uniforms. Please send money home urgently, the letter read, before the power is cut off. Dieter sighed. He would have to go to the post office after lunch once he had organised the boys. There he sent a postal order and a brief message:

Hope you are all well. Your son Dieter.

After dinner at night the day was still young and they decided to visit the Melanesian hotel. Roy, Dick, Ian and Dieter sat on sofas furnished in floral fabric set around a low table. The white walls and ceiling gave the feeling of light and space. Polynesian waiters took their orders where they sat. No need to go to the bar. SP was the drink of the day, beer brewed by South Pacific Breweries in Lae.

Back at the quarters they agreed it was a pleasant way to end the day. They sat on the veranda upstairs overlooking the Huon Gulf. There were tall palms wandering back and forth in their line of vision as they inhaled the scents on the night air and listened to the sounds. Frogs and crickets competed with each other.

"There goes the 'plying bokis'," Roy said imitating the way the locals pronounced flying fox. The young men laughed as they headed off to their rooms.

CHAPTER FIVE

"Want to go to the market?" Darrel poked his head around the bulk store door. Dick was there too.
"Sure thing. It's not too busy today." Dieter replied.
In the morning he had watched the people, brown backs glistening in the sun, as they paddled their canoes laden with produce up to the beach. Coastal schooners also came in with people and wares. Sepiks with wooden carvings filed off the Sumiho tied up at Voco Point wharf. Some of the people were met at the wharf and piled onto trucks, their 'wantok's kar', to be taken to market. Meris came from nearby villages carrying goods in string bags on their heads, often with another bag on top of everything else holding the baby. The town bustled and buzzed like this each Friday.

The market was set up on the perimeter of the showgrounds not far from the single men's quarters. The sun shone on the iron roofs of the stalls. It was shady underneath but would get hotter as the day wore on. Bamboo stands were set up underneath and people busied themselves, getting everything out for sale. Some sat on the ground in front of the stands with more produce around them. Myriads of dark skinned people of varying hues chattered excitedly. The place was crowded. Here and there a European head was visible above the throng. Dieter was amazed as they wandered through. A greying man with thickly curled hair bent over a log chipping away at a carved mask under a tree. Carvings of crocodiles, seahorses, masks, a low crocodile coffee table. There were even stuffed crocodiles.

"How much?" Dieter asked pointing to a magnificent carved seahorse.

"Ten dolla, masta."

"Okay." Dieter handed over the money. He would send it home with other pieces that caught his eye. Mutti could keep them for him till he got home again. Tucking the seahorse under his arm he carried on. At the next stand were small green strands of berries. Dieter wondered if they were immature coconuts.

"Now that's buai, betel nut," Darrel explained. "And these," he said pointing to little boxes made of banana leaves, "contain the lime. That's how you get all the red stains on the ground, like blood, where they spit it out."

"Does it taste good?" Dick wanted to know.

"Not especially but it gives them a bit of a kick. It's a mild stimulant when they mix it with lime."

"But why do they need to spit it everywhere," Dieter went on. "That's revolting."

"It evidently gives them a guts ache if they swallow it," responded Darrel. "And it makes their teeth and gums red."

"Yes but it can also eat away at their gums too."

A woman with a red grin held some up to Darrel.

"No thanks, not today."

There were dead birds for sale. And possums, lizards and flying foxes. Some had been wrapped in clay and cooked. A couple of birds were split open to show their tasty innards – all well cooked. Further on they had snakes, some cooked, some still alive. The larger living specimens were bound onto a long bamboo stick, tongues flicking in and out at all the tasty smells around. Bamboo cages held smaller snakes. A man stood behind the stall with a python wrapped around his chest and its head held firmly in his hands.

"Why don't you try that?" Dieter said to Darrel.

"I have. Why don't you?"

The man obligingly unwound the snake and gave the head to Dieter to hold. "Keep arms up," he said gesturing to Dieter like a chicken flapping.

Dieter raised his arms as the keeper made sure the snake entwined his torso under his armpits but not his neck. The snake's head felt like a dog's but it was cold.

FLIGHT TO FREEDOM

"Thanks. That'll do! Dick wants a turn." Dieter was keen to pass it on.
"Not on your life. But I enjoyed watching you," he said.
"Chicken," Darrel chided.
Next they came to the fruit and vegetable stands. Coconuts were lined up with the green shell husked.
"Three please," Darrel held up three fingers. The young man cut the tops off three coconuts and handed them over. Darrel paid up. It was a refreshing drink as they ambled along. Such delicacies Dieter had never seen or tasted before – mangoes, papaya, guavas, star fruit. Then there were bananas, watermelons, rock melons, oranges, lemons and pineapples.
"So cheap," said Dick. They all agreed.
"What's your favourite, Darrel?" Dieter asked.
"It has to be mango."
"Okay I will start with a mango, see whether I like it, and some bananas at that price."
Further on were vegetables – taro, yams, onions, potatoes, cabbage, tomatoes, carrots, lettuce and beans.
"I would have thought it was too hot to grow these here," Dieter said.
"Yes, but they are grown at Sattelberg, about 3000 feet above sea level. It was the first mission station set up in New Guinea by the German Lutherans in 1892," Darrel explained.
"So that is where Mrs Fugmann was brought up," added Dieter.
"Yes, her father was the second missionary there."
"That's amazing," Dick said.

The young men ambled along. They did not need to buy household supplies. That had been done earlier by Darrel and the cook boy. The fish section was next. Everything was very clean. A young lad holding a palm frond in each hand fanned the parcels of fish wrapped in banana leaves, to keep them as cool as possible and the flies away. Buyers were shown the contents of one parcel at a time which was then wrapped and tied again to keep it fresh and moist. On to the clothing section where women sold meri blouses, laplaps and clothing they had made. Darrel held up a length of tropical patterned cotton.
"Anyone want another laplap?" he asked.

"No, not today," Dieter replied. "I've spent enough for one day, but I'll be back."

"I'm right too," said Dick.

The boys wore laplaps instead of shorts in the evening when they relaxed - it was much cooler - but not when the young ladies visited.

"Well that's about it," Darrel said as they headed back to work.

"Thanks for showing us around," Dick responded. "You wouldn't starve here, would you."

"No, but there are some things I would never eat even if I was starving," quipped Darrel.

CHAPTER SIX

Sunday afternoons were always quiet and relaxed. Sometimes they went swimming but today Dieter had planned to get plants for the garden he had been creating around his 'home'. They could do with some indoor plants as well. After lunch and a siesta while the cook boy cleaned up, Dieter, Dick and the cook set sail in the landcruiser. Dieter knew where to go. He had seen colourful plants as they drove past what everyone called Hospital Hill which had been honeycombed by the Japanese as a hideout during World War II. Dick parked the vehicle in front of the Chinese shop where they had bought their fans as new arrivals.

It was a pleasant walk meandering down the old track. They found colourful crotons which some of the villagers used instead of trousers, sliding the stalk under the string belt around their waists. In the front over the belt they wore a loin cloth, woven from bark string. This left the buttocks and thighs exposed. It was cooler and not restrictive like the white man's clothes. Cheaper too! In Pidgin English crotons were called 'as gras'.

"We'll have some of that," Dieter pointed to a variegated devil's ivy as it twisted and twined around the trunk of a tree. He watched a brilliant blue butterfly flitter past. What a haven of peace. This garden would exceed what he had done in Wangaratta. Much easier in the tropics.

"Yu laikim masta?" the cook boy asked, a leaf of a fruit salad plant in his hand.

"Yes good. Let's take this lot back to the truck."

They loaded the coffee sacks and went back for more. Dieter, keen to brighten up their accommodation, was oozing enthusiasm. Rays of sunlight streamed over the thick growth and onto the path as they began to descend again. Dieter was leading the way, striding out when suddenly he stopped. There on the path in a patch of sunshine was a shiny blue-black snake uncoiling and getting ready to strike.

"Hell!" Dick said bumping into Dieter as he turned to run. The cook boy won the race back to the truck. The tranquillity had been shattered.

"I think that will do," Dieter said between gasps as they clambered into the truck. "We got some good specimens."

Later Dieter talked to a group of locals about their experience. He was keen to know what kind of snake it was. One of the men was a director of Namasu and head man of Butibam Village.

"You were lucky," he laughed. "Didn't you know there are still many Japanese in that hill. You shouldn't have gone up there. It's off limits to everyone."

"I didn't know," Dieter said.

"Well I guess you won't be going back."

CHAPTER SEVEN

"You might like a change of scenery," Mr Fugmann said. "The Sio is going to Finschafen to take supplies. It leaves at 10 pm Friday night."
"Yes we'd love to go," Dieter and Rick answered. Hans was keen to join them too. So it was set up with the missionaries at the station.
It was a clear night as they left the wharf at Voco Point. Tom, a native skipper, with sound knowledge of the coast, was at the helm. The moon shone down on the water lighting their path.
"You don't get seasick?" the skipper joked.
"No I will be right." Dieter was confident. "It's a calm night so I'm sure there will be no problems."
Hans had been brought up in New Guinea so he was used to coastal travel.
"Just stay behind the cabin till we get clear of the channel," Tom said. "I need to see where I'm going."
Dieter looked at the lights on the cross arm of the mast. They did not seem to give off much light but he had obviously done it many times before. The diesel engine chugged along powering the boat through the water. The supplies were stacked in the hold for the missionaries at Finschafen and Sattelberg and merchandise for the trade stores in the region. The ocean's smell mingled with the diesel fumes when Dieter stood near the stern of the boat. He knelt down, bent over the side and trailed his hand in the sea. Moonlight shimmered on the ripples as the boat slid through the water. A lone seabird called in the distance. This is the life thought Dieter. He had never dreamt it could be so sweet just over a year ago.

"We're fine now," called Tom. He handed each of them a rug. "You can sleep on the deck under the stars." They sat around and chatted for a bit and then settled down, each wrapped in their blankets and their own thoughts. A gentle breeze ruffled Dieter's hair and the motion of the Sio soon lulled him to sleep.

At first light Dieter stretched and sat up. The night had been surprisingly comfortable. A hazy glow on the horizon heralded the coming day. He saw lights bobbing on the water.

"Just watch," Tom said. "You'll be able to see them soon."

As the sun rose above the edge of the sea the lights from the tilley lamps were extinguished and gradually they spied fishermen in canoes. Out fishing all night. The sound of conch shells came from all directions, some near and others far, as the men called to the village folk that they were on their way home. Life was simple and uncomplicated for them. Full of beauty and meaning. Dieter hoped he could portray what it was like in a letter to Opa.

By 6 o'clock they were tied up at the Finschafen jetty. Here they were met by Ted who took them to the mission house for breakfast

"We'll see you tonight," Ted said after breakfast. He and his wife Miriam had managed the hospital in Finschafen for many years, she as a nurse and he as maintenance cum handyman.

Back at the beach Hans, Rick and Dieter were shown to two outriggers pulled up on the beach. After greeting them the strong native men began to paddle them out to Tami Island. The water was crystal clear with myriads of rainbow coloured fish darting hither and yon as the canoes sliced through the water. Some were an iridescent blue or green. As they circled to the north of the island to slip through the coral reef into the lagoon Dieter marvelled at the starfish and seahorses languidly going about their daily routine. They seemed oblivious to the fish darting around them and the shadow of the canoes passing overhead. It had taken an hour to get from the mainland to Tami and at last they drew the canoes onto the beach, stepping out onto dazzling white sand.

The village crouched on the edge of the beach where the lush vegetation started. The houses were built on stilts about three feet off the ground. They were made of natural materials with kunai grass roofs and woven pitpit walls. Coconut, banana and betel nut palms stood tall among the huts. Pigs snuffled round throughout the village looking for tasty morsels under palms. The villagers smiled and

greeted the young men in Pidgin as they were taken on a tour. Children scampered around the new arrivals while a man with a red betel nut grin acknowledged them and continued whittling at a tall mask. Outside the village neatly fenced gardens had been cleared. Sweet potato vines wandered amongst plants of sugar cane and elegant taro leaves nodded at them.
"How about a swim?" Hans asked when the tour had finished.
"Sure," Dieter and Dick agreed.
Leaving his shirt and thongs on the beach Dieter ran down to the water's edge and dived under the water.
"Come on," he called to the others as they waded in. "It is not cold."
Soon they were fooling around in the lagoon inside the reef with lithe naked bodies of village children streaming past them underwater. With arms by their sides they looked like seals searching for fish. They started a game of underwater chase.
"You catch me," they challenged the visitors. With that they dived below and swam away like slippery eels. Soon the young men came up gasping for air. Eventually the children came to the surface laughing.
"They've had plenty of practice," Hans said.
"Yes and they dive deep," Dick added. "If I could hold my breath as long as them I reckon I'd catch them."
   In the end after much fun and rollicking they gave up and sat in the shade on the beach.
"Yu laikim papaya?" One of the women came and offered the prepared fruit on a banana leaf. "Mi go kisim dring," she said as she hurried off. Soon she reappeared with coconut cups full of 'wara bilong kokonas'.
"Certainly very refreshing," Dieter said.
They chatted with the locals and talked about their lives. Fishing, carving, trading. Dieter found it interesting to see first-hand how they lived. While not much food could be grown on the island they carved canoes, masks and dishes out of wood, trading them at markets on the mainland. Fish was a major part of their diet and could also be traded.
   Dieter enjoyed the peace and calm of the island. He could not help contrasting it with the life he had lived in Australia. Only occasionally did he think of his family there. It all seemed so long ago now. But he hung tenaciously to his memories of Europe and the

people he had left behind. They mattered more to him than anything else. So the day went on. A swim in the lagoon followed by another snack of sweet potato cooked in the ashes or some pineapple cut lengthwise into segments. In one of Dieter's forays underwater he found a conch shell near the reef. He came up for air, took a deep breath and dived down to the sea bed. It was a beauty – the fish inside had gone and only the tip of the shell had been broken.
"Must have been tossed over the reef by a huge wave," Hans said as he turned the conch over in his hands, stroking the smooth surface, his fingers following the spiral. "I'll show you where to drill the hole if you like. When we get back to Lae."
"That'd be great," Dieter replied. "Then I could join a conch band."
Hans laughed. "I reckon that it'd more difficult than you think."
"Count me out," Dick joined in. "I haven't got a note of music in me!"

By mid afternoon it was time to make the return trip to the mainland. They said goodbye to the villagers, thanking them for the delicious food and their kindness. Tousling the fuzzy hair of the children, they promised to come back when they could hold their breath better.
"We'll catch you next time," Hans said.
The children laughed.

Once back at Finschafen it was time for coffee and cake. They chatted about Tami and how they had not been successful catching the local children under water.
"I am not surprised," Ted said. "They learn to swim almost before they can walk."
"I'd like to go for a walk," Dieter said as he finished his coffee. "Wander along the beach while it's still light. What time is dinner?"
"Plenty of time. We don't usually eat till 6.30, do we Miriam." Ted looked to his wife for confirmation.
"That'll be fine. We'll see you then."

Dieter breathed in deeply as he wandered along the shore. He scrambled down the rock wall and walked along the beach, carrying his thongs so that he could feel the sand on the soles of his feet. The sun had started its downward glide to bring warmth to other parts of the globe. It would be summer in Germany now. Would the sun's rays be reaching Opa yet? Give him a kiss from me when you get there, Dieter said as he turned to meander back. Small shells dotted the beach with a conglomeration of them crowding the crevices along the rock wall. The tide was out but no doubt the waves lapped against the wall at high tide, unloading treasures. Further along by the grey volcanic rocks of the wall he noticed a white craggy rock at the base. Dieter was curious to examine the stark contrast. Moving it with his foot he realised it was a large snail shell. The inhabitant had long gone and the shell showed calcium deposits of smaller creatures which had lived on the outside. The inside was mother of pearl and Dieter could only imagine how the shell would look once it was cleaned and polished. The calcium coating was very thick and Dieter could not see any cracks. He took it down to the water to rinse off the sand on the outside and anything that might be lurking on the inside. Back at the house before dinner everyone admired Dieter's find.

"It'll be hard work but take it slowly and you could have a real beauty," Ted told him.

"You are getting quite a collection," Rick said.

"I wasn't really looking for them. They just turned up," replied Dieter.

After the evening, relaxing and getting to know each other, Ted invited them to go to Sattelberg for church in the morning.

"We'd love to," they replied.

"You can have a look around and we'll tell you some of the history. It's quite impressive," Miriam added.

"How far is it?" Rick asked.

"It takes about an hour. Don't worry, we'll get you back in time for lunch. You won't have to walk back to Lae. The Sio will wait for you," said Ted with a grin.

"Right-o then."

The next morning after breakfast they piled into the jeep and headed off to Sattelberg. The road wound up and away from the coast through thick rainforest. Cuttings through rock and clay enabled the jeep's three thousand foot climb. Sattelberg with its cooler climate was where some of their vegetables came from. At last the bouncing on the back of the jeep lessened as the road flattened out and they pulled up outside the church. It was a huge edifice built of corrugated iron left over from the Second World War.

"But I'll tell you about that later," Ted said as he began preparations for the church service.

Two square towers stretched heavenwards, standing guard over the front door of the church. Louvres high on each side of the towers sheltered the bells, remnants of the earlier German missionaries. From there the call rang out to come to worship. The door to the church was ornate by New Guinea standards with carved wood attached in the form of a cross. Crosses adorned the tops of both towers and the roof peak. The church itself was long and tall but what was most surprising to Dieter was the fact that the whole building was clad with corrugated iron. Even though the church stood at three thousand feet above sea level in the tropics it seemed an incongruous choice of building materials. He hoped the louvre windows under the eaves would allow the air to circulate so that they would not roast in the pews.

The three young men survived the service in reasonable comfort and afterwards Miriam and Ted took them for a walk around Sattelberg.

"As you would expect this part of the mission was pioneered by Germans from the Neuendettelsau Mission in Bavaria. Consequently in 1939 all the men were rounded up as Nazi sympathisers and interned in Victoria at Tatura. Their wives and children left the territory later but they were permitted to live with friends or family in the community. However the women informed the authorities that they too had Nazi leanings in order to join their husbands in the camp. Then in 1947 Willie Bergmann returned to Finschafen."

"But why the corrugated iron?" Dieter wanted to know.

"Well the Japanese invaded Finschafen in 1942. They were forced back by the Australian forces and retreated to Sattelberg. In the following battle that ensued bombs were dropped around Sattelberg but the Japanese had already gone," Ted went on. "When they were finally routed in late 1942 a trail of death and destruction was left behind. Willie Bergmann returned to find bomb craters and ditches, some with hand grenades and live ammunition in them. In these areas he would light a fire with grass and twigs then skedaddle till everything had exploded. He rebuilt Sattelberg using the remnants left behind from the war."

"The Americans walked out and left so much," Miriam put in. "Vehicles, machinery, corrugated iron and other building materials which they considered useless."

"Willie's first job was to make a mission house habitable so that he could rebuild the mission station. The Sattelberg church is a living memorial to Willie's hard work, courage and tenacity. Of course it will last longer than the former church built of kunai grass and pitpit matting," Ted concluded.

"What an amazing story," Rick replied. "A mission station rebuilt from the detritus of war."

After lunch that afternoon Dieter, Rick and Hans returned to Lae on the Sio. Tom the skipper had enjoyed the weekend with his family and the young men had a new appreciation of the trials the early missionaries had encountered during World War II. As they skirted the coast they were all lost in thought. Dieter was a very young baby when the Japanese invaded New Guinea en route to Australia if all had gone to their plan. By the time Willie Bergmann arrived to put everything to rights at Sattelberg, Dieter had been uprooted from his home, wandered as a refugee around Germany with Opa and Oma and was finally settled in southern Germany. It seemed to him that it did not matter which side of the world you were on at that time in history, it involved hardship, torment, death for some and struggles which gave way to new beginnings.

CHAPTER EIGHT

Ever since arriving in Lae Dieter had heard about the show held in October each year. For the past two weeks the showgrounds had been a hive of activity. Firstly huts from different tribal areas were built. Then people from outlying villages began setting up displays, as well as business people from Lae with food stands and agents advertising vehicles and machinery for those who could afford them. On Friday Dieter went past in the Namasu truck.
"Lukim masta," Marame said. "Show i kirap!"
"Mi laik lukim," Dieter replied.
"Orait yumi go tumora."
"Good!"

On Saturday morning Marame met Dieter at his quarters and they set off. Toby and his family, dressed in trade store clothes, were already at the show. Having lived in Lae for some time and worked for the white man it was easier to buy meri blouses and laplaps or cotton shifts for the women and girls, shirts and shorts for the males. Toby had been educated in English too so they set off together.
"Let's go up the tower first," Toby suggested. "Then we can see everything and take photos if you like."
The tower was a tall flimsy looking contraption built of timber and bamboo with cross struts bound on with rope to give the semblance of stability. Three ladders end to end were strapped on and gave access to the basket like platform at the top. A rope ladder could be used to climb up on the other side if one felt exceptionally daring. Guy ropes from all directions kept the construction vertical and

eliminated most of the swaying. A flag fluttered from a pole above the heads of the three sightseers who were up there already.

"Right you are," said Dieter. It seemed strong and many people were making use of it. The queue was not long at this time of day and soon it was their turn to clamber to the top.

It was a fantastic view right across to the trees and homes on the other side of the show. In the grounds were round houses built of woven pitpit walls and conical kunai grass roofs. The corrugated iron shelters of the market were incorporated in the broad ring of buildings circling the grassed area for the demonstrations of culture – singsing competitions. The most spectacular building had been erected by the people from the Sepik River area. The grass roof was a diamond shape with a horizontal ridge along the middle for most of its length. The shorter sides of the diamond pointed to the ground while those in line with the ridge turned up to face the blue sky. At each end of the building there was a matting porch held up on posts. The angled side posts of the building supported the roof. The lower part of the side walls were an open basket weave. Above that was reinforcing mesh with netting over it to let in the light. Dieter wanted to check that out when he was on solid ground again. A myriad of people thronged the areas between the buildings, some in traditional dress, others in European clothing. Black umbrellas shaded many of them from the sun. Pale skinned Europeans stood around in clusters or meandered through. Dieter took snapshots to send south and then carefully backed off the platform to make way for the next sightseers.

As they wandered around the huts Dieter was able to glimpse how different clans lived. Wantoats showed how they cleaned kina shells used for trading, even for buying a wife. Some cleaned coffee beans, others honed stone axes and bound them with strong flattened vines to a wooden handle. Women made string for carry bags –bilums for a baby or produce from the garden. If they needed to carry vegetables and the baby, two bags were required with the baby's bilum on top! In the Sepik house woodcarvers whittled masks, statues and animals such as crocodiles and fish. Women wove bilums using fingers and toes to make the net bags. Dieter marvelled at the skills of these people. He could also see the influence of the white man as coloured wools were integrated with possum fur and bark string.

"Let's look at the dancing," Toby suggested when they had moved right around the display huts.

"Yes, they are all under way now," Dieter noted.

"This is a competition," explained Toby. "Today is the preliminary round judged by the Assistant District Commissioner. Some will be called back tomorrow for the final and the District Commissioner will judge them."

"But they are all so different. How on earth do they judge it?" Dieter was stumped.

"Oh they judge on dress, their rhythm and loudness," Toby explained. "One group at a time performs on the oval and when they move off the next one comes on."

First up was the group from the Morobe District holding wooden A-frames that held tall tapa sails aloft over their heads. Feathers adorned their heads with leaves, bones, shells and woven bark string loin cloths on other parts of their bodies. They chanted and moved to the beat of the kundu drums held in their hands. Two elders of the Morobe clan watched nearby, dressed to the hilt so that scarcely any skin was showing. Next came the Sepiks. Some of the men were dancing while others were re-enacting a human sacrifice to the crocodile god. A tapa cloth covered the crocodile frame with grasses hiding the limbs of the man inside as the beast glided across the grass. A doll representing a pikinini was visible in its mouth to show that it meant business.

Dieter moved in to take a close up shot of the Hube warriors. The head dress was adorned with cockatoo feathers and the pulpuls covering their loins were dyed and multi-coloured. Suddenly he realised that he was encircled when another group came in from behind to cut off the enemy. A hand grabbing his shoulder made him jump. With relief he saw it was Roy from Namasu who pulled him to safety.

"Even though it is a mock battle with the drums beating and the men chanting it induces a trancelike state. You need to stand well clear and not get in the way," he said.

"Thanks I'll remember," Dieter replied sheepishly.

Wantoats had cockatoo feathers round the edges of their headgear. They had red feathers and dark ones arranged to look like fearful faces. Their traditional dress was dark in comparison.

"Imagine just the head gear poking up above the top of a mountain on a dark night," Toby joked.

"Rather not," said Dieter, "it might give me nightmares!"

Garaina tribespeople were led onto the ground by two men playing bamboo flutes. They wore white loincloths with leaves rustling and bird of paradise feathers nodding atop their large wigs.

"The wigs are made of human hair," Roy said, "maybe from their mother in law."

"How do you know," Dieter laughed as the rest of the group hustled after the leaders.

Later the group walked back through the crowds to the haus tambaran. Dieter and Roy had some serious haggling to do for carvings. Although there were always carvings at the market there was more variety and many more carvers to barter with here. For now Dieter would enjoy them in his room but he intended to ship them home to decorate his abode wherever he ended up when he left New Guinea.

CHAPTER NINE

High in the cab of the Osh Kosh Dieter had an expansive view of the countryside as he left Lae. He had been asked to fill in as manager at Goroka while the incumbent went on four weeks annual leave. Dieter had been in Lae almost 18 months and knew the workings of Namasu and what was expected. He was looking forward to a new challenge. Next to him sat Jimmy with Dan, the truck owner, at the wheel.

"So how long have you been travelling the highway," Dieter asked Dan.

"Oh I started out as a kiap with the Australian government. I did that for several years until I bought this beast two years ago."

"You like this job better?"

"Hell yeah," Dan replied. "Nothing beats being your own boss. Got to keep your wits about you though. Watch out for slips. And robbers. That's why I've got me mate here, eh Jimmy."

Jimmy grinned, his white teeth standing out against his dark skin.

"Yes Dan. We catch 'em."

"Jimmy is a good driver too so he can take over for a bit."

"That's great!" Dieter commented.

The tarseal road was straight as they headed out past Nadzab, the airstrip used by American and Australian forces during World War II. The strip had been recently resealed as an alternative to Lae when weather conditions were bad. It was plain sailing as they left Lae then Nadzab behind and continued up the Markham Valley. Here the corrugations in the dirt road juddered through the chassis into the cab. It would make my teeth rattle, Dieter thought, if my mouth was open.

The Valley was wide at this point as the Highlands Highway and the Markham River ran side by side. The highway ran straight with economical purpose up into the highlands in the name of progress; roads slicing through the country, up and over mountain passes, linking tribes who had never known the others existed before the white man came. The 'knowing' was not always peaceful. The river meandered along the Valley taking as much space as it desired on its way to the Huon Gulf.

"How long to Goroka?" Dieter asked Dan.

"About four hours on a good day," he replied, "taking into account the stops."

The truck growled as Dan took it through the gears on the approach to the bailey bridge. It was one way only and seemed to go on forever.

"How long is it?" Dieter wanted to know.

"About a third of a mile. Put in during the war and very handy. I guess they will have to replace it one day but it's still strong."

The bridge rattled as they drove across. Dieter caught triangular glimpses of the river on the way over. On each side of the valley was grassland stretching as far as he could see. A good source of building materials for the village people. Kunai for the roof and pitpit for the walls.

"So where do we drop off cargo," Dieter asked. He knew what they had loaded but he had never been up the highway before.

"Kainantu's first, then Hegenofi and finally Goroka. We'll have a bite to eat at Kainantu."

It was difficult to talk over the noise of the engine as they began to climb and leave the river behind. The road meandered, twisting and turning as it climbed toward the Kassam Pass.

"Magnificent view," Dieter commented as he looked on the clumps of trees dotted on the hillsides. Here and there villages clung to the side of the mountains with gardens supporting their way of life.

"Yes but you'd need to be a mountain goat to live here," Dan laughed.

"What's the altitude?" Dieter wanted to know.

"We are not there yet, but the Kassam Pass is just over 4900 feet above sea level. Then we're in the Eastern Highlands," he explained.

Shortly the road levelled out onto an undulating plateau with a vista of vast grassland appearing around them. There was a government station over by the airstrip.

"That's the ADC's house over there and a couple for the kiaps too," Dan said. "There is the haus sik." He pointed to the aid post where the locals could get rudimentary first aid. The only vegetation apart from grasses was a few straggling yar trees around the prefabricated houses where the government officials lived.

"Here we are," Dan announced as they pulled up outside Namasu Kainantu. Jimmy jumped down and called out to the store boy to open up the bulk store next door.

"We'll leave them to it while we grab some grub and stretch our legs," Dan said. They wandered into the trade store and collected a tin of bully beef each and one for Jimmy.

"A packet of sao crackers too and three bottles of Namasusu," Dieter said.

Dan took out his army knife and opened the cans of beef. Dieter and Dan took chunks of meat, pasted it on the crackers and began to eat.

"Not my favourite meal," Dan said, 'but it keeps me going till I get home to the missus and a meal fit for a king."

Dieter nodded. He had heard that Dan was married to a coastal girl and wondered what a meal fit for a king would be like in Dan's home.

When the truck was unloaded and Jimmy had a bite to eat he took over the driving as they headed for Hengenofi. Dieter noticed gorges running like giant cracks slicing through the western edges of the plateau. He imagined what would happen in a downpour but presumed that any villages would be built out of the way of frequent deluges. Henganofi was similar to Kainantu only smaller. It was also an administrative centre of the Australian government with a contingent of European kiaps, a native dokta boy and polis boys. A Lutheran mission station had been built since the Second World War. Dan pointed it out to Dieter as they pulled up at the Namasu store on the main road. Once they had unloaded supplies they were off again to Goroka.

Heading west out of Henganofi Dieter could see how the land dropped away from the plateau with more gorges carving up the landscape. In the distance Mt Michael rose out of wispy clouds in the valley below, its summit gently rounded with bushes and vegetation.

FLIGHT TO FREEDOM

"Looking forward to your stay in Goroka?" Dan asked breaking the silence.

"Yes it'll be good experience I think," Dieter replied.

"You'll find they are a different mob, but you'll be right."

"A month is not long and then I'm back to Lae," Dieter said.

Goroka was the main administrative centre of the Eastern Highlands, Dr Fugmann had told Dieter. Not nearly as big as Lae but it had a large Lutheran mission and high school there called Asaro.

Approaching Goroka Dieter spotted the traditional territory administrative centre that had been set up – offices for the district Commissioner and his contingent of kiaps who patrolled the outlying areas, carrying out a census for the Australian government, maintaining law and order, hearing court cases, polis boys who attended to minor matters; dokta boys with a rudimentary level of first aid to run the haus sik. There was also a United Nations hospital at Goroka to see to the more specialised health needs of the Indigenous and European population. The hospital had been established in response to the quest for answers to kuru disease which was endemic among the Forè tribe.

On past the town, they drove for several miles on the main road towards Asaro. At last they pulled up outside a corrugated iron bulk store with a sign that read 'Namasu Goroka.'

"Here you are," Dan said. "Jimmy can unload while you put your bag in and have a look around your digs." Dan pointed to a door on the end of the bulk store. Dieter was soon unpacked. His accommodation was an open area with partitions separating a shower and toilet space from the bed/sitting room and the kitchen. He wandered outside to look around. The landscape was barren compared to Lae although he could see tall mountains in the distance.

"See you next time," Dan said as he climbed into the cab for his return journey to Lae.

"Yes," Dieter responded, "whenever that will be." Dieter turned and went into the bulk store where he introduced himself to the head boy, his offsider and a driver boy. There was no trade store attached here as their role was to supply goods to trade stores and mission stations in the area. The yellow and black Land Cruiser parked by the bulk store would be used for this.

While in Goroka Dieter went out into the hinterland to extend Namasu business amongst the many villages. On his first trip Dieter was feeling his way. He wanted to please Dr Fugmann, show him he could be relied upon to do a good job. Out past Goroka they veered off to the right and wound down towards the western side of Mt Michael. Dieter had a strange feeling, did not feel entirely comfortable as they wove their way toward villages close to the road.

"Stap plis," Dieter instructed the driver as he noticed a native fellow watching the truck approaching. "Mi laik tokim dispela man."

The man had mossy creepers wound around his head, a traditional bark string loin cloth hung in front from his belt with tankets (a bunch of crotons) at the back. His bare chest and face were decorated with clay stripes. Dieter wound the window down in spite of his hostile appearance and talked to the man while the driver boy translated from Pidgin into his local language. He was not helpful, maybe he spoke a different dialect. So they drove on past the bush clad mountain on one side and rolling country with kaukau mounds on the other. Soon they turned around and drove back – he would try a different area another time.

Dieter found life in Goroka depressing. One thing could be said for the weather here – it was usually predictable with high hills and ranges protruding out of fog in the valleys into clear sunlight in the early morning. In the afternoon clouds formed on the ranges and heavy storms often followed. But it was a lonely place with no one living nearby. At night it was very dark with no street lights and Dieter felt uneasy. The head boy in the bulk store resented Dieter being there and wanted to be the boss. Dieter suspected that pilfering was going on though he did a stock take and kept track of inward and outward goods. The wash boy assigned to wash Dieter's clothes had stolen some. Cooking his own meals was no fun and not as palatable as meals in Lae.

'What has happened to paradise?' he asked himself. Life in Lae had seemed like a holiday in comparison. No wonder his colleague needed time out. Dieter would be pleased when his month was up and he could return to Lae to enjoy Christmas festivities there with friends and company his own age. He had another six months of his contract left and hoped he could remain in Lae.

CHAPTER TEN

Dieter had settled into life in Lae again when one day Dr Fugmann turned up at the bulk store and took Dieter aside. "There is an urgent job for you in Kundiawa. Can you be ready in an hour? I have just arranged a flight. We can talk on the way."

"Right," Dieter said. His stomach did a flip. He hoped it would not be like Goroka. He wondered how long he would be there. It was the beginning of March now, just a few more months to go. What was going on? Why the haste?

"I'll pick you up at 10.30," Dr Fugmann added.

Dieter walked back to the single men's quarters, past the garden he had created, up the stairs and into his room. He had no time to say goodbye to anyone. Surely his boss would let the others know. Opening his drawers Dieter soon packed his neatly folded clothes into the suitcase. Sliding hangers across in the wardrobe he took everything except the winter woollies he had arrived in. He smiled at the thought of it. They could stay there until he went south again, whenever that would be.

Right on 10:30 am Dr Fugmann pulled up in his Mercedes. He opened the boot so that Dieter could stow his suitcase.

"We'll be on our way then." He put the car into gear and they headed for the airport. A Cessna 185 stood on the runway, Dave the pilot waiting beside it.

"You're travelling light," he said to Dieter.

"Don't need much in this climate," Dieter responded.

"It'll be cooler where you're going."

"Much the same as Goroka I would have thought." Dieter could not believe it would be any different. He had popped a jumper in for the evenings just in case.

"No probably not. Well climb in and we'll take off," Dave said.

Dr Fugmann and Dieter sat behind the pilot and fastened their seat belts. They could talk and Dave would not hear over the noise of the engine. He closed the door then clambered into his seat. Soon all checks were carried out as the engine roared and they trundled out for takeoff. It was a sunny day and flying would be great, Dieter thought, in spite of the fact that he did not really want to leave Lae so soon.

"This is what has happened," Dr Fugmann wasted no time once they were airborne. "Herbert has upset people in Kundiawa, many people."

Dieter had met Herbert once when he came to Lae. He was the manager of Namasu Kundiawa and was responsible for buying coffee beans from the native growers as well as managing the bulk store.

"He has tried to impose his ways on the people. His standards and traditions. One of the tribes, the Sina-Sina, are very hotheaded and they are threatening to kill Herbert."

"Lucky you found out." Dieter was aghast.

"Yes! They sent three of their headmen to talk to me. All the way on a wantok's truck. I knew we must not waste time but attend to this immediately."

"I understand." Dieter nodded his head.

"So here we are. Herbert will have to leave, come back to Lae when he has shown you what to do. He will not return."

Dieter nodded glumly.

"You must stay until I can get a replacement," Dr Fugmann continued.

"Yes I will do my best," Dieter replied.

"You must move cautiously not to make the situation worse."

Dieter was shocked to know why he was needed. His experience in Goroka served to inform him that this was not going to be easy. He would need to be firm with them but fair.

Dieter gazed out the window at the terrain below. He watched the plane's shadow as it scudded along just to the left of them. The route had followed the Markham Valley but now the plane was climbing as they approached the mountain range. Just as Dieter thought they did not have the altitude to make it, an updraught lifted the plane up and over the crest and let it out of its grasp to fend for itself on the other side. Dieter glanced at Dr Fugmann.

"Don't worry. That is how it goes in a small plane – lift on this side, drop on the other," Dr Fugmann said smiling. It was Dieter's first flight in a small plane.

He continued his pondering of the Kundiawa situation. It was like one culture trying to dress up the other by overlaying their values, he thought. Just like he had seen in Australia with the aborigines in one place. It never worked! It caused heartache and hatred. What about Europe? Although Dieter was very young during the war he remembered when they fled their home and wandered through war torn Germany till they settled in Bavaria. He thought of Oma and Opa. How they had pieced together their lives. That's what he would have to do! Like making a patchwork quilt. Taking the good things from both cultures and creating a thing of beauty, something practical for both sides. Yes, that is what he would try to do.

On the ground in Kundiawa they were met by Herbert and taken into his office. Dr Fugmann wasted no time in coming to the point in his forthright manner.

"Never mind what has happened," he said to Herbert when he tried to explain from his perspective. "The situation is very serious and this is what we must do."

So Herbert was told that he must show Dieter the ropes and introduce him to key people as quickly as possible. Then they must pack up with extreme haste and fly out to Lae.

"I will arrange a plane for the end of the week. Does that give you enough time?" Dr Fugmann added.

"Yes," Herbert replied. "My wife has already started to pack."

"Good. I advise you to stay in Kundiawa from now on. Give Dieter a list of his duties and all the trade stores and coffee plantations on the books. It would not be safe for you to travel on the roads."

Herbert looked as though he was about to say something but Herr Fugmann held up his hand.

"Enough! We must not waste time. I am sorry it has finished in this manner, but we cannot afford to wait and see if these people are serious. I am sure your wife would agree. Now I must see how they are going with loading the plane. We will take what coffee you have."

Dieter moved into a sleepout behind the manager's house until Herbert and his wife left. He was pleased it was not attached to the bulk store. Herbert introduced Dieter to the staff, gave his opinions of them and could not help trying to justify his actions. Dieter listened but decided to make up his own mind about what needed to happen later.

At last the couple was safely away and Dieter was his own boss. As he began his day with a shower – a bucket and shower-rose job on a pulley – he thought about breakfast. Coffee will do just now. I'll have something to eat later, he told himself.

CHAPTER ELEVEN

It was not easy as Dieter settled into his new job and tried to make peace. He decided to take things slowly. Strengthen relationships and get everything running smoothly at the Kundiawa base first. That would allow time for word to filter through that Herbert had gone and a new 'masta' had taken over. Today he was travelling to some of the outlying areas. Just after daybreak he headed out on the Highlands Highway with Joseph the driver boy. After a short distance they turned off and wound along the steep side of the Chimbu River valley. Mist meandered through the valleys at this time of day. Later it would dissipate as the sun warmed the valley floor. Clouds would roll along the peaks in the late afternoon, often followed by a storm. Dieter had soon learned the different weather patterns here.

Now the sun was peaking over the tops of the mountains but the red clay road shaded by the steep mountain sides would not feel its warmth till about 11 o'clock. The fecund smell wafted to Dieter's nostrils as he wound the window down and breathed in the fresh air. The cruiser, which could only grind and crawl along this road, was loaded with bags of rice and tinned fish for the small trade stores they would service along the way. It took all the skill and concentration of the driver to negotiate the winding, bumpy, slippery road that sloped towards the ravine in places. Their arrival in the area was announced by bush telegraph. Villagers along the way raised their arms above their heads and called a sing song message with a rising 'oo-wa' on the end. Thus everyone was alerted long before the truck arrived.

Dieter had already dropped off a load at one trade store and was headed for Genabona, a village set back in a place where the hills opened out. As they approached the village a group of six men gestured for them to stop. Dieter and the driver climbed out to talk to them but it soon became obvious that this was not a friendly welcome as the ringleader began harassing Dieter, ranting and raving. He took a bone knife from his bark belt and pointed it at Dieter's chest. Another two men joined the group as Dieter turned round to gain support from Joseph but he had fled the scene. These people were not his wantoks and he feared for his life. At this point Dieter decided the safest thing to do was back off and not antagonise them. Now another man with red clay painted on his cheek bones moved forward and quietly gave orders. To his horror all Dieter could do was watch as they started pushing his vehicle sideways towards the edge of the road and then over the bank. He was sure that as it gathered momentum it would end up in the river far below. Dieter's adrenaline kicked in and now it was his turn to be angry. His eyes popped wide open as he eyeballed the perpetrators. He waved his arms and gesticulated in an effort to make them understand. Now they would have to look after Dieter, give him something to eat, he mimed, and somewhere to sleep. It would take him days to walk back.

Then the red clay man shouted to his cohort, who drew machetes from their bark belts. Keeping an eye on them Dieter sidled to the side of the valley. He peered over and there was the landcruiser caught on a crazy angle by a large stand of bamboo about halfway down with the cargo intact. That was all very well but how would he ever get it up again. Looking back to the men he saw they were cutting tall thick bamboos from the other side of the road. Red Clay sorted out two men to begin pounding the bamboo with stones while the others chopped more sticks. Soon they all joined in the pounding while Dieter continued to berate them. He was very angry and would not give them an inch. What a nerve! It appeared he was safe in the meantime but he had to keep up the pressure while he was ahead.

At last the driver came back.
"Em i orait, masta," he said as he watched the group twist strands together and knot the thick pliable bamboo rope into one length.
"All right? It's not all right!"
"You watch, they will pull the truck up onto the road."

Dieter stared in disbelief as the whole tribe materialised out of the bush and joined in the process. With Red Clay shouting instructions and one or two others putting their bob's worth in, they scrambled down the hillside and secured the ropes round the land cruiser. What followed was a great deal of pushing, heaving, shouting, dragging, grunting, more shouting, gasping for breath, puffing and panting. With a final shout of triumph, somewhat muted because of lack of breath and the energy they had expended, the truck was hauled back onto the road. It seemed no worse for wear and the cargo on the back was intact. It must have slid sideways down the moist slope. Dieter would not have believed it if he had not been there. But what would they demand now for their efforts? Dieter did not feel inclined to trust them anymore. Red Clay pointed to Dieter and then to the truck.

"Let's go," he said to the driver.

With a wave they drove away, gingerly, until they proved that the steering was intact and functioning well.

"What was all that about?" Dieter asked his driver. He shrugged.

"Mi no save toktok bilong em," he replied.

The perpetrators were from a different tribe and consequently spoke a different language. They decided to carry on delivering goods as it was impossible to turn the vehicle around on the narrow road. Later the deceit of the Genabona people turned to respect and they were the best of friends. A trade store was opened there and Dieter chose a Catholic layperson from the village to manage it.

Omkalai was their next stop. They dropped the store supplies there without incident and headed back to Chimbu. It had been a disturbing day! Once they had unloaded the cargo Dieter decided to visit the Lutheran mission, pop in for a cup of coffee and a chat.

"How lovely to see you," they said. Dieter enjoyed calling in and they always made him feel welcome.

"So how's it going?" Bob asked when they were seated round the table with coffee and biscuits in front of them.

"Very frightening this morning," Dieter said as he recounted his tale. "What I don't understand," he went on, "is why they changed their tune and hauled the truck back on the road."

"You must have looked scary," Bob's wife suggested.

"Scared, more likely," Dieter responded. "I couldn't understand them and I doubt they understood my Pidgin by the look of them. Perhaps when I gestured they would have to feed me they thought I was going to eat them."

CHAPTER TWELVE

Another day Dieter went to Kerowagi, just under an hour's drive, on the Highlands Highway. It was a civilised place compared to some of the others he visited and the store was well stocked to compete with Brian Heagney, the other trade store owner there. Of course it was a well populated area with many outlying villages. The Dangga people lived in the fertile plain where the Wahgi Valley opened up. They were a prosperous and peaceable tribe, their land dotted with gardens of subsistence farmers as well as tea and coffee plantations. Kerowagi was a pleasant trip after Genabona.

"Good morning." Dieter greeted John the store boy.

"Good morning masta."

"How is it going?" Dieter surveyed the store. Everything was neat and tidy. He was proud of John as he had proved to be reliable. Tins of mackerel, bully beef and Peking duck, complete with bones softened in the canning process, adorned the shelves, bags of rice on the bottom shelf with packets of biscuits beside them – sweet biscuits, sao crackers and hard cabin bread. Salt, sugar, lolly water and tea above. Further along there was clothing and manchester neatly displayed, shorts, shirts and belts for the men, brightly coloured meri blouses, gathered skirts for the women, strings of small coloured beads, Barilla soap, talcum powder which often ended up on the baby's head, hair oil, brushes and combs, towels, grey cotton blankets and balls of wool. On the adjacent wall the shelves held lamps of two varieties (tilley and hurricane), aluminium saucepans of all sizes, cutlery, enamel teapots, cash boxes and padlocks. Diverse uses had been found for padlocks. Besides securing your property, as long as it was not in a shed made of flat iron which could be opened with a tin opener while leaving the door securely bolted, some men thought a padlock was an attractive adornment to hang from their nasal septum or ear. Next to the padlocks were stick tobacco, matches and newspaper to roll your own. Long curved strips of metal, called sarifs, were available, useful for clearing unwanted vegetation from a new garden patch. Tomahawks and bush knives, used to cut pitpit and kunai grass for house building or for harvesting sugar cane, lay on the shelf. In the wrong hands they could be used for more sinister purposes.

"Plenty business but not much rice and mackerel left," John said.

"Good work. I'll do the inventory first and see what else you need."

It took a while to do the inventory and reconcile the money in the cash box but Dieter enjoyed coming to Kerowagi where John listened to him and was constantly increasing sales and profits.

"Right-o John, here's the list of what you need. We'll get it from the truck," Dieter said at last.

Joseph jumped onto the deck of the truck and slid the cartons down to the end so that John and his helper could cart them in. Dieter ticked them off the list as they went.

"Well done," Dieter said as he shook John's hand. "See you next time."

Dieter was looking forward to getting home early as they climbed into the truck and set off for Kundiawa. I reckon a coffee and a cigarette while I read my book and watch the sun go down will be a treat tonight, he said to himself. Although there were Europeans on the government station at Kundiawa he had not had much to do with them. When he first arrived they were not friendly and so they had a nodding acquaintance only. He missed the camaraderie that he had experienced from people his own age in Lae. But as time went on he did not hold out much hope of returning to Lae to work.

CHAPTER THIRTEEN

Dieter's working life in Kundiawa consisted of delivering goods to outpost trade stores and buying coffee beans to backload to the bulk store for transport back to Lae on the Highlands Highway. There the beans were processed by Namasu at their factory. This routine was interspersed with staying at the base when the Oshkosh was delivering goods each week. Apart from that his social life was almost non-existent.

The driver boy and Dieter left Kundiawa as the sun rose. It would be a long and arduous trip that would take up most of the day. Dieter wound down the window to breathe in the fresh morning smells. Once they had left Kundiawa behind the road led along a gorge between razorback mountains. It had been cut into one side of the mountain, about half way up. Dieter lit a cigarette and puffed contentedly as Joseph took control of the vehicle and the road. He was very experienced and Dieter was thankful for that as he surveyed the mountains above and below them. This was not a trip for the fainthearted. There were towering rocky outcrops demanding attention as they stood out amongst the mountain rainforest of the Bismarck Range. Down in the bottom of the gorge there would be a river running swiftly no doubt, not that Dieter could see that far. He was content to know they were travelling along a solid yet narrow and torturous road with an excellent driver at the wheel.

It had been frightening the first time he had travelled to Gembogl. The driver was obviously accustomed to it and had not bothered to elaborate on what he was doing. At one point right on a bend the road had been blasted through rock. The tray on the land cruiser was almost the same width as the cutting through the rock. This and the fact that a sharp left-hand turn was needed immediately after the manoeuvre, made it a doubly hair raising experience.

"Sapos mi go isi isi trak i pas," the driver had said when they were safely around the bend. Dieter's eyes had nearly popped out of his head and he had hung on for dear life as the driver had paused to put the truck in low ratio and then gunned the engine to ensure they got through the gap, suddenly swinging the steering wheel to the left. The sounds of the engine revving reverberating off the rock and the tray scraping through left Dieter gasping.

"Why didn't you warn me?" Dieter asked the driver.

"Sapos mi tokim yu olsem, yu pret nogut tru." He looked across at Dieter to see if he was angry.

"Bel bilong mi i olsem kabis," Dieter responded as he let go of the passenger door and let out his breath. "Rot i orait nau?"

"Yes em i orait..... liklik," he added with a grin.

Having travelled round the Chimbu frequently Dieter knew what he meant. The worst was over until on the way home!

The rest of the journey was uneventful by comparison and after four hours on the road Dieter was glad to arrive and stretch his legs.

"Let's have lunch first and then we'll unload," Dieter said to the driver. "We have got plenty of time."

Lunch usually consisted of sao crackers and bully beef brought from home and a bottle of water. Dieter was dubious about bringing sandwiches because the meat might go off in the heat. He unwound the strip on the can and pulled the lid back. He dug out a spoonful of the meat and scooped it off on the cracker. Not bad for a quick lunch he thought as he stretched his legs under the dash.

Once lunch was finished he went over to the trade store. He hoped word had got out that they had arrived and the storekeeper would be there. The first task was to do an inventory of what was left of the stock brought by Dieter last time. Then he would ask for the key to the cash box and do a tally to see the money balanced. It was not often that it balanced in any of the stores. Dinas (loans) would be given to wantoks and the storekeeper might take items out for his own family. Sometimes records were kept if they had had the privilege of attending a mission school. If the difference was not too

great Dieter would explain once again that the amount they were short would be taken out of the profits at the end of the month.
"Yes Masta. Mi save."
"Orait yu mekim kamap olsem," Dieter repeated.

Next he supervised the driver boy to get what was needed from the truck to restock the shelves.
"All right! We'll have a carton of fish, two bags of rice, three meri blouses and some sugar and tea."
"Is that all?" his boy replied.
"Yes, there's not enough money in the cash box for anything else. He'll have to get the money his wantoks owe him."
At the conclusion of the business transactions it was time to socialise with the people who had turned up to talked to Dieter or to cadge a lift back to Kundiawa with them.
"Sikispela man, em inap," Dieter told them, as he was taking most of the cargo back with him today.

It didn't take long for the lucky six to clamber up leaving the disappointed ones behind.
"Your turn next time," Dieter said to them in English and they seemed to understand. Small naked children ran beside the truck as it left in a cloud of dust to get back before daylight waned. The men on the back chattered in their own language and settled back to enjoy the trip. Dieter looked at the mountains around him and wondered if ever the books would balance in the trade stores. How long had they lived among these mountains without roads, just mountain tracks, keeping to themselves in case the tribe over the range took a pot shot at them with a bow and arrow? It was such a short time in comparison since the white man had brought new ways to them but were they better ways? A mere thirty years was hardly enough time to transition if they so desired. Mick Leahy had been the first white influence in the area in 1933 he had been told.

Tapping on the cab roof reminded Dieter where he was in time and place.
"Mipela laik go daun," the spokesman said.
"Orait," the driver said as he slowed the truck.
It was interesting Dieter thought. Never did they go all the way to Kundiawa. He wondered if they had heard tales of the frightening bend through the rock passage. Daylight was fading fast by the time they arrived back at base. The day had been long and arduous, like

the road. Going to the kitchen cupboard he selected his dinner. Tonight it was a can of Irish stew with a couple of slices of buttered toast. A shower first to remove the day's dust and then he could relax.

CHAPTER FOURTEEN

Dieter enjoyed going to Bundi, a village set on the side of Mt Wilhelm which towered above it to a height of well over 14,000 feet. Bundi was an outpost of the Catholic mission at Keglsugl. As there was no road access Dieter had to fly there in a small Cessna. The plane left again as soon as it dropped Dieter off. The weather near Mount Wilhelm was unpredictable and clouds could close in quickly leaving the plane stranded. The first time Dieter had flown empty with the single engined plane that seemed to hop over the ranges and drop on the other side as it headed for the airstrip. He was there to negotiate with the people to see if they would like to run their own trade store.

It was a good sized village and the people were totally different from the Chimbu tribe. They were tall and mild-mannered seeming more like a Polynesian race. Today he was going there to service the store with supplies. It would be necessary for him to stay overnight as the plane would not be back till morning. As the plane circled round to come in to land at the entrance to the airstrip Dieter marvelled again at the neat layout of the village in a horseshoe shape around the strip, leaving the entrance clear. Palms and other tropical trees surrounded the village. A walking path wound down to a tributary of the Ramu River. A short way down, Dieter had been shown previously, was a lush area with a gushing waterfall cascading into a crystal pool. This was where they washed each day and Dieter found it much preferable to his bucket on a pulley shower in

Kundiawa. While he was there they offered him food and never asked for payment as some villages were inclined to do.

Dieter was pleased to note that the store had been a great success, with the village being overseen by the Catholic mission. This village was like an oasis for him in an arid desert devoid of much social interaction. Once he had seen to the store and spent time with the storekeeper he went to make his bed. The beds he stayed in had been carefully made by attaching split bamboo poles to a framework. The bed here was at least long enough for a European. The problem was that the flat side of the bamboo was down to make it easier to fasten to the bed frame. The curved side was the part on which Dieter rested. The uninitiated would wake up in the morning after a fitful sleep with a corrugated backside. So Dieter always made sure that he prepared his bed, well before the afternoon rains came. He cut an armful of kunai grass, which grew plentifully everywhere as it was needed to thatch their houses, laying it over the bamboo. He was an old hand at it now and enjoyed a very comfortable night's sleep. He always felt refreshed after a visit to Bundi.

CHAPTER FIFTEEN

The next morning after Dieter flew in from Bundi he sauntered over to the Namasu base at Kundiawa. The distinctive yellow painted building with black trim stood out in the sunlight. Maremi the boss boy of the complex greeted him. It was good to have reliable staff, Dieter mused as he surveyed the young men filling orders in the bulk store while Maremi checked them.
Beside the bulk store was a smaller office wedged in between the bulk store and trade store.
"Morning Masta." The store boy gave Dieter a wave.
"Morning." Dieter gave him a smile as he unlocked the office. On the desk inside was a letter from Jacob. He opened it. Good! Jacob had been sent to Gembogl to get the finances in order, get payment for the debts that the store owner there had incurred by giving his wantoks goods without payment. Jacob had managed to turn it around, get cash for the goods taken on credit and make it profitable once more. Dieter would need to go to Gembogl tomorrow to collect the cash and see if he could find someone suitable for Jacob to train. Jacob was needed back at Kundiawa. He had been educated to high school level at a mission school and was responsible for keeping the books and counting the cash while Dieter was away. Although Jacob came from far away his clan had links with Gembogl so it would not be difficult to get a good replacement.
Off at first light the next day, Dieter hoped to get there and back in the one day. He had work to catch up back at base, and inventories to reconcile and monthly reports. The devil's elbow on the Gembogl

road no longer fazed him. He was pleased with Jacob and what he had achieved in a relatively short space of time. No doubt he would be needed to troubleshoot somewhere else, but in the meantime he would have the team complete in Kundiawa. So Dieter thought as he leaned back, surveying the ever-changing scenery quite relaxed.

When they arrived however, the store was shut and locked. No one was to be seen. Joseph called out the way they all did to make the sound reverberate off the mountains.

"Jacob-o..... (Then words spoken quickly in his own language that Dieter could not understand)...... Jacob-o-wah." No response at first so Joseph tried again. At last one of the village men approached them.

"Jacob, em i stap?" Dieter asked.

"Asde, em i go pinis." He smiled revealing a gap in his teeth, happy to be able to help with the information.

Dieter nodded as he took out his keys and unlocked the store. It was unusual that Jacob would write a letter and then take off on other business before Dieter arrived. He hoped he was all right.

"Bilong wanem, em i go?" Dieter asked the man.

"Mi no save."

"Em i orait," Dieter replied. He shut the door behind him as he went in. On the top shelf behind the saucepans he felt for the cash box and took it down. When he opened it he found there was not a brass razoo! The $1000 was not there. There was something fishy here! If there had been a break-in Jacob would have reported it, but he had run off. Dieter did a quick stock take of the goods in the store. He needed to ascertain how much was missing. He picked up the cash box and went out, locking the door behind him. The sun beat down on Dieter and Joseph as they walked through the village talking to the villagers but no extra information was forthcoming. Dieter had a feeling they knew what was going on as they were not their usual friendly selves. With a heavy heart Dieter climbed back in the truck with Joseph for the return trip.

As soon as he arrived back Dieter let himself into the office. He needed to find out the true state of affairs, see how much money and stock was missing. He checked the stock against the last inventory. From his office records he checked the list of credit that had been given to wantoks at Gembogl. When the sun had set and he needed a Tilley lamp to see, he toted up the money in and money out. All in all

Jacob was $1000 short – exactly the amount he suggested Dieter come to collect. But why would he do that? He had always been trustworthy. His tribal elder was a Lutheran pastor, well respected by the community and the church establishment. What had gone wrong?

Next morning Dieter went to the assistant district commissioner (the top government official in Kundiawa) to report the theft and the fact that Jacob had gone bush.

"My apologies Dieter but I am unable to do anything about it just now. I'm up to my eyebrows with the Sina Sinas. If I can't get them to settle down there will be a right royal blood bath," the ADC said. "How about you go to the magistrate and he'll help you sort it out."

Dieter was unsure about that, but the longer he left it, the less likely they were to get their money back.

"You need to apply for police powers at the court for this case only. Then you are able to pursue and arrest the thief," the magistrate advised.

Although he did not feel like it Dieter set sail for Gembogl at once, this time with a police boy. He decided that they were more likely to find the miscreant at Gembogl with his clan's trading partners than home in his own village of Kerawagi. But he was not there. Word travelled by the bush telegraph faster than a brown-breasted high titter or a bird of paradise could fly. They spent the rest of the day wandering around talking with the locals, then bedded down for the night.

Next morning they left. There was no point in staying, they told the locals. Dieter, the police boy and the driver sat in the cab discussing the case. The three of them were sure that the locals knew where Jacob was, maybe they were hiding him. As soon as they came to a wider place in the road the driver backed and tacked until he had turned the truck around and drove quietly back to the village. Sure enough, as the truck pulled up they saw Jacob disappear into a house. Houses having only one door was a drawback for his escape. He was quickly apprehended, handcuffed on the back of the truck and on his way back to Kundiawa. There he was handed over to the magistrate and put in jail till his court hearing.

Jacob would not talk when he stood in front of the magistrate. He would not say where the money was, so he went back to jail while more enquiries were made. The magistrates suggested Dieter go to Jacob's wantoks in his own village and talk to his immediate family.

At first Dieter went to the Lutheran pastor who was in charge of the other native pastors in the Chimbu district. No, he knew nothing about it. However when he approached others in the village they said that several of the family had gone to Lae. He would need to come back when they returned in three or four days.

Now Dieter was really suspicious. Before his wantoks came back and while Jacob was still languishing in jail Dieter received a telegram from Dr Fugmann:

Take no further action stop Tribal elders insisted stop Jacob gave them $1000 stop Threatened to withdraw their shares and embargo all Namasu stores in area stop Loss suffered would be far more costly stop
Fugmann

The tribal elders came back with a new white truck, paid for in full with the final amount provided by Jacob. Jacob went back to his village and did not get another job. He reverted to his tribal customs, turning his back on the opportunities he had gained through his education.

That evening Dieter sat down and reviewed his situation. He felt angry about the time and effort he had wasted and the fact that Jacob and his wantoks got away with it. Admittedly Jacob had lost his job but had maintained his standing in his community. Dieter could do nothing about that but he had become disillusioned with life in Kundiawa. His contract for two years work in New Guinea to all intents and purposes had finished in July, over two months ago.

"Kaikai redi, Masta," the house boy said as he placed Dieter's dinner on the table. Tonight he had given the boy rice to cook and two tins of MaLing duck to heat up, as well as the obligatory cup of coffee.

"Thank you," Dieter said. "Good night."

"Good night Masta," he said as he left.

Dieter pondered some more. He knew that if he brought up the matter with Herr Fugmann he would urge Dieter to stay in Kundiawa. That was where he was needed. Fugmann kept his eye on the new recruits in Lae and transferred them to the outposts as the need arose. Dieter had no chance of being transferred back to Lae where he had had company his own age and a social life.

Finally Dieter made a decision. He would leave Namasu and return to Australia, perhaps Darwin. He certainly did not plan to go back to Wangaratta and live with Mutti. That option was not enthralling. She still sent wheedling letters to him asking for money but those he could put aside till he was ready. At least he did not have to face her each day. After all the years of servitude to his mother he wanted to enjoy life and be able to put money away to return to Germany and Opa. But first he wanted to go and see the Mount Hagen show. He had heard about it from so many people. 'It needs to be experienced,' they said. 'Mind you it's very different from Lae.' So Dieter requested time off work in October and the use of the truck (and driver boy) to go to the Hagen show. He had taken no holidays at all, so he was entitled to do that. It would be a change of scenery and he would have time to think and plan.

CHAPTER SIXTEEN

It was the beginning of the wet season in October 1969. Dieter and Joseph left in the four wheel drive at eight in the morning bound for Mt Hagen. The show was held every second year so Dieter was glad to be able to see it before he left New Guinea. He had timed it just right. The unsealed road twisted and turned until they reached Kerowagi. It was a good road by New Guinea standards compared to the Gembogl road. At last they reached the wide open Wahgi Valley. As they rounded the last bend the plain stretched before them. There was no breeze to cool the merciless sun that beat down on them at this time of day.

Dieter stretched his legs and relaxed in the passenger's seat. He glanced down at his tanned legs pockmarked with scars left behind by leeches and all manner of insects. There was no doubt that his lifestyle in the Highlands had left its mark. Whenever he scratched his leg on anything he seemed to get a tropical ulcer that took forever to heal. It had not happened in Lae when he had an abundance of fresh fruit and vegetables and fish in his diet. He would be fine once he got back to Australia he decided.

Surveying the countryside he saw glimpses of villages further back off the road in stands of yar trees for shade and protection. Mounded kaukau gardens were dotted here and there with some being tended by women clad from the waist down, leaning over the hillocks as they weeded or planted new tubers, their bare breasts dangling as they hoed.

"Have you been to Hagen before?" Dieter asked Joseph.

"Yes only once," he replied.

"What's it like?"

Joseph shrugged his shoulders.

"Colder than Lae with different people. They fight with each other. Not like Lae."

Dieter nodded. He had been told that although the Leahy brothers, Mick and Dan, had trekked into Mount Hagen in 1933 after gold, there had not been a major influx of Europeans into the Highland interior until the 1950s. Mick Leahy had long gone but Dan had stayed and become a plantation owner, marrying native women from two different tribes. Later his children were to recount how they had watched tribal warfare between their two mothers' tribes from the vantage point of their veranda. It was a spectator sport they said, with clubs and spears being wielded with skill. Dan had been a notable influence in the area, always being careful to treat both tribes equally. Of course there was an airport at Mt Hagen now and the Highlands Highway ground its way up from the coast. Phenomenal progress had been made since the Leahy brothers first appeared and the local populace had treated them with great respect due to them thinking they were long lost ancestors who had returned with white skins. Tribal warfare and payback killings are still a part of life to this day although the white man is treated with respect, the Catholic priest had told him. Now he was going to see for himself.

 Dieter was in a contemplative mood as Joseph negotiated the Highlands Highway en route to Mt Hagen. He had enjoyed life in Papua New Guinea – the coastal people, tropical lifestyle of Lae, being away from the constraints of Mutti. There was no doubt that he would be sad to leave. Back in Australia he would need to go to Wangaratta first to collect his belongings and the carvings he had sent home, but he did not intend to stay there. It would be asking for trouble even in separate accommodation. Where would he go? Maybe Darwin would be good. He had no wish to settle in Sydney but Darwin would suit him well, as far away as possible from his mother.

"How about a stop," Dieter suggested to Joseph as he came back to the present.

"Orait," Joseph said as he pulled off the road beside the deep ditch that was necessary in times of a tropical downpour. They both had a smoke and a drink of lolly water, stretching their legs before they continued.

An hour later they arrived at Mt Hagen singsing ground where the show was held. The unsealed road of the Highlands Highway led them to it on their way into Mount Hagen. It was a large open space at the end of the Kagamuga Airport. Dieter marvelled at the kaleidoscope of colour from the distinctive tribal head dresses made from human hair and decorated with bird of paradise plumes, fur from the cuscus and flowers. The long feathers nodded as the men walked along, their loincloths swaying in front and croton leaves (aptly known as 'as gras' in pidgin) rustling over their backsides. Having been in the truck for so long Dieter decided to stretch his legs. See what was happening.

"See you back at the truck later," he said to Joseph.

"What time?" he asked.

"Around 3 o'clock," Dieter responded. "So that we get back before dark."

"Orait masta."

Dieter wandered round the stands looking at the carvings, woven bilums and other handcrafts but he saw nothing that he had not seen before in Lae. Then too it was more difficult to get things through customs as a passenger travelling back to Australia than by post as he had done several times now.

Down the end of a row of stalls he noted a stand with Waso printed in red letters above it. Dieter went to investigate.

"Hello," the man said in an American accent.

"Hello," Dieter responded looking at the display of photos. It appeared that Waso was carrying out a similar line of business to Namasu.

"So what brings you here?" the man asked.

"Oh I've been working at Lae and in the Chimbu for a company called Namasu. I am about finished my contract and wanted to see the Hagen Show before I go south again."

"Well I am Ed Dickie by the way."

"I am Dieter Klier." Dieter shook the hand that Ed held out in greeting. "So who runs Waso?" Dieter asked.

"Funnily enough Waso is also run by a Lutheran mission, the Missouri synod from the US."

"I've heard of the Missouri synod before but not Waso," Dieter admitted. "But it looks as though you do much the same as Namasu." He pointed to the photos.

"Yes we do. So what were you doing in the Chimbu?" Ed queried.

"I was running a branch there – overseeing trade stores in outlying areas, training storekeepers as well as managing the bulk store and ordering supplies, doing stock takes, buying coffee to backload to the factory in Lae."

"You wouldn't be interested in a similar job for Waso, here in the Highlands?" Ed asked.

"Well yes I'd think about it," Dieter said. "I don't really want to go back to Australia just yet but I'd like a change of scenery. Where would it be and what would I be doing?"

"Look come in and have a seat. Would you like a cup of coffee and a slice of my wife's pumpkin pie while we talk?"

"Yes thank you." Dieter was dumbfounded. Maybe this was the answer to his dilemma.

Over coffee and pie Ed explained that Waso was expanding into the Enga province. Waso had just bought a trade store with a large bulk store behind it and a house on the second floor. They were looking for a manager, Ed said. After he had shown Dieter where it was on a map and they discussed the role and pay he could expect Ed turned to Dieter.

"Well what do you think?"

"I'll take it," Dieter responded.

"How soon can you start?"

"I'll have to go back to Kundiawa first and then Lae to finish things off and hand over but I should be able to come back within a couple of weeks."

"That'll be good. I'll see you when you turn up at Wapenamanda and we'll take it from there." They shook hands on the deal and Dieter went off to continue his tour of the show.

His mind was in a whirl as he stood and watched a tribal group doing a singsing. It seemed such a coincidence that he had come to Hagen to say goodbye to life in New Guinea and a new and unexpected door had opened for him, leading him deeper into the Highlands to a more remote area. But he was open to the challenge. Give him a chance to experience another part of New Guinea. Put off going back to Australia, facing his mother and all that would entail. Dieter continued on past the various stands. The district commissioner's display showed a model of the Highlands outlining the projected roads and their progress in the district. There were maps on sale so Dieter bought one of his new territory. Nearby was the agricultural officers' display of coffee growing in the area, all owned by Europeans but crucial for building up the economy in the region. Dieter bought some Hagen coffee. The police were there to ensure harmony prevailed amongst the tribes. Further along was a first aid post set up by the Haus Sik contingent.

Following his nose Dieter pursued the smell of Aussie barbecue right at the end, standing alone but by no means lonely. He would grab something to eat and then watch the enchanting displays. The Hagen Pub Kaikai had a variegated crowd mingling around it. Dieter joined the queue and watched as he waited his turn. Triumphant customers came away with handfuls of sausages wrapped in bread, tomato sauce beginning to drip from the ends. Some managed a cold beer as well. Tourists, with cameras hanging round their necks, milled around. They had spilled out of the DC-3s that had been landing and taking off all morning it seemed since Dieter had arrived. There was limited accommodation in Hagen – just the Kimininga Hostel and the Hagen Hotel – and it would no doubt be chocker block. He watched bemused as a peaked-capped American gesticulated to two groups of people bedecked in costumes to move closer while he took a photo. It was obvious to Dieter that they were from two distinct tribes and he hoped they were friendly. They were not! But fortunately one of the men made that clear by waving his spear in the tourist's face and showing his contempt for the other group. Dieter breathed a sigh of relief as the photographer got the message and settled for one group at a time.

With two bottles of VB in his knapsack and three sausages encased in bread, Dieter headed for the singsing ground where all the competition took place. He found a leaning post on the fence that circled the area, shaded himself and the pack on his back with an umbrella and began to eat. Around him the New Guineans sat on the ground. Dieter did not fancy doing that because many spat as they sat around waiting for their wantoks to perform in the competitions. Best presented group, most colourful young unmarried meri, fiercest looking single male, then the singsing itself based on rhythm, chanting and dance. The district commissioner was the judge ably assisted by his ADC. They sat in a grass roofed shelter halfway along the oval grounds.

As he watched Dieter looked around him and spotted Roy who had lived in the single men's quarters with him in Lae.

"You are a long way from home, aren't you?" Roy joked.

"Not as far as you?" Dieter replied.

They sat and chatted about what they had been doing and Dieter could not help telling Roy about his good luck in stumbling onto a new job that day. Roy still worked in Lae in the office at Namasu or in the coffee mill. Occasionally he was required to pilot a plane when Dr Fugmann chartered one.

"I missed the company of you blokes when I went to Goroka and Chimbu," Dieter explained.

"Can't say I'd like to work there either. Now here you are among some of the tribes you will be dealing with."

"Wish I knew who was what!"

"That's easy," Roy went on. "You know the Chimbus of course. That group over there with wide wigs like an A-frame are Huli. They border onto the Enga province. And there is an Enga with the rounded hat with bird of paradise feathers dancing on top."

Time flew as Roy pointed out people from the Jimi Valley, Lake Kutubu, Hagen and many other places, discernible by their getup but also by facial features and their build.

"Thanks Roy. It's been great meeting up with you again, but it's time I was leaving. Joseph's around somewhere and we want to get back before dark."

"I don't blame you. I am staying overnight with friends. All the best in your new job. Hope it goes well," Roy responded.

CHAPTER SEVENTEEN

Dieter had a lot to think about as Joseph drove them back to Kundiawa. He would get a flight to Lae as soon as possible to see Dr Fugmann and finish up with Namasu. While there he would visit his mates at the single men's quarters and collect the rest of his property that he left there. He would not say a word to his staff in Chimbu until it was all organised. Back home that evening after dinner Dieter's thoughts turned again to his new position at Kandep. He hoped to have more company there, that Kandep was more than just a government outpost. Ed had seemed confident that there were business opportunities there and money to be made. He would give it his best shot as he always did and see where it took him.

Two days later Dieter took a TAA flight to Lae. Pleasant memories came back to him as the small Cessna circled Lae, over the single men's quarters and the beach at Voco Point, to land at the airport. He would have been quite content to stay in Lae. His first stop was at Dr Fugmann's office where he was welcomed with a firm handshake and smile.

"So why are you here?" Dr Fugmann asked after the preliminaries. He was not one to make small talk while he waited.

"I've been offered a new position with Waso in the Highlands and decided to take it," Dieter said. In spite of rehearsing what to say in the plane, he came straight to the point like his boss.

"I see. When will you begin this position?"

"Not until I have settled up with Namasu," Dieter replied.

"That is good. I have a replacement in mind. Please stay tonight and I will let you know in the morning."

Dieter was relieved that it had been that easy. He wandered through Lae and back to the single men's quarters. He looked across to Hospital Hill and thought about his narrow escape with a deadly snake, all for the sake of some plants. Down at the wharf the Sio was being loaded to take goods down the coast, probably to Finschafen or beyond. But now he was moving on to pastures that were greener than Chimbu he hoped. The next morning following a pleasant evening and dinner with the boys and a cold beer or two at the Melanesian for old times' sake, Dr Fugmann met with Dieter again.

"Dick will be your replacement," he said. "He will leave with you at 11 o'clock this morning. I have organised a flight."

"Thank you."

"Once you have explained everything to Dick and done a stock take you are free to go."

Dieter nodded. He was confident that Maremi, his boss boy, had everything in order and under control.

"I wish you well and hope we may meet again if ever you are in Lae," Herr Fugmann continued.

"I will," Dieter said. "I am grateful for the opportunity you gave me to come here."

"You have done a good job. May God keep you in his care."

Back in Kundiawa Dieter soon completed a stock take with Maremi and Dick to help.

"You're a lucky one," Dieter said to him, "being able to stay in Lae all that time."

"Oh, I believe in doing my job, but not so well that the boss takes notice of me," Dick said with a grin. "It was your own bloody fault! You work too hard."

"Is that right? But now I'm out of it and you are my replacement. So that'll teach you for being so smart."

Dick slapped Dieter on the back. "That's all right mate. I was only joking."

Over the next couple of days Dieter outlined his schedule to Dick, telling him when he went where. He did not think it was necessary to take him to the outlying villages where he did business. Dick had been in New Guinea as long as Dieter and knew the running of Namasu inside out.

"Joseph is a good driver. He is reliable but I will need him for a couple of days. Herr Doktor said he can take me to Wapenamanda."
"Righty-oh! That'll give me a chance to get to know everyone here before going bush."

CHAPTER EIGHTEEN

So Dieter was off on the next phase of his life. He felt exhilarated, in control again. Thinking back to when he left Australia, it was that same emotion as he headed into unknown territory. He was not afraid, he was excited. This time his mother was not looking over his shoulder, telling him he would fail. Those times had long gone but still they had left their mark.

The road to Hagen was familiar as Joseph drove Dieter along the route they had travelled ten days previously. Joseph glanced across at Dieter as he said, "I will miss you masta."
"I will miss you too. It was time to find another job."
"Masta Dick, is he a good masta?" Joseph asked.
"Yes he was a good friend to me in Lae. He will be a kind boss if you work for him like you have for me."
Joseph grinned then. "Em i orait masta."

Dieter and Joseph were not prepared for the road past Mount Hagen where the Highlands Highway had finished. It was a treacherous road that twisted and turned climbing up the Hagen Range towards Kagul Pass at over 9000 feet above sea level. The dirt road clung to the hillsides as the truck tried to avoid the potholes. Bridges consisted of tree trunks as bearers, with smaller branches tied on with bark rope. On top of this layers of mud were caked, which was a good thing in a way as Dieter and Joseph could not see the health of the woodwork underneath. It would be some years before the Highlands Highway ventured forth into this rugged territory. They followed the valley formed by the lower hills in the mountain range. These all converged on the valley floor to dip their feet in the Lai River and tributaries.

"Olsem wanem? What is this?" Joseph asked as the truck jumped, rocked and bounced over the terrain.

"We'll have to go easy, easy," Dieter replied, "if we want to get there in one piece."

Joseph stopped and put the truck in high ratio as they continued on. Now he understood why they had marsden matting on the back of the truck – in case they needed to do some bridge repairs. This road was not much more than a one lane track. So far they had not met another vehicle on the road and it certainly did not look as though it was used much. At least they should see a cloud of dust if a vehicle was coming towards them. If it was coming up and over a hill it would probably be crawling like them.

By mid afternoon they were forced to stop as they watched rain sweep along the valley to engulf them. The downpour was heavy with low visibility. Dieter and Joseph sat in the vehicle hoping it would pass as quickly as it had arrived. At last it was gone but it had left behind a slippery clay road with evil intent. Progress was now even slower as Joseph endeavoured to keep the truck away from the sudden drops over the edge. Dieter thought the sides fell away about 100 to 200 feet, not that he wished to have a decent look. Waterfalls gushed down ravines where before it had been a peaceful and serene setting. Finally they had to give up and call a halt. Although they were over the Kagul Pass and heading towards Wapenamanda darkness was creeping up on them.

"I think we should stop," Dieter said at length. "We don't know the road and now it's getting difficult to see."

"Yes," agreed Joseph.

They slept in the truck as best they could and carried on at daybreak. It was a relief to arrive safe and sound at Wapenamanda.

"Welcome to the Western Highlands." Ed shook Dieter's hand. "Just in time for breakfast."

"Thanks," Dieter replied. "We thought it best to sleep on the road after the rain came and then it began to get dark."

"Good move." He had nodded in approval as he saw how tired Dieter looked.

"How about we find somewhere you can have breakfast, a shower and catch up on some sleep."

FLIGHT TO FREEDOM

Dieter nodded. It had been a cold night and Dieter had not felt entirely safe being in an unknown area. After saying goodbye to Joseph as he went off to be fed by a Waso local driver, Dieter was driven to Mambisanda nearby where a Lutheran missionary couple took care of him. Breakfast and a wonderful shower, then into bed. He was amazed at the accommodation the American missionaries had, compared to the Australians but he was not complaining. He soon succumbed to the comfortable bed. It was arranged that he stay the night there too, going on to Kandep the next day.

Next morning he was up bright and early and back to Wapenamanda to meet with Ed and talk about his responsibilities in Kandep. Ed talked about his vision for Kandep. Dieter would buy produce from the locals and send it back to Wapenamanda. There was also a government initiative to establish the growing of pyrethrum daisies in the district thus supplying the natives with a cash crop. Then the Engas would have money to buy shares in the Waso store, making it their store and thereby building up the economy in the region. Dieter was enthused. Whatever needed doing, he would do it. He had never been afraid of a bit of hard work. While in Lae he had proved his mother's predictions to be wrong. Ed would be pleased with his achievements.

"Might as well have some lunch before you set off," Ed said, when at last he finished the session with the book-keeping side of the business and reporting back to base. Dieter agreed.

In the meantime his four-wheel-drive was being loaded with supplies for the Waso store in Laiagam on his way to Kandep, as well as some for his own branch.

"This is Timothy," Ed said introducing Dieter's new driver.

"Hello." Dieter shook his hand. "Pleased to meet you."

"He's been driving for us for some time and he's an excellent driver," Ed went on.

"That's good. He'll know the road then."

"Yes he knows it well to Laiagam and he's driven to Kandep once. Took your furniture over the other week."

"Aha!" Dieter nodded.

It was a mild afternoon and the sun was shining. Cicadas played their percussion instruments in the bushes. Ed saw Dieter off with an encouraging slap on his shoulder. Dieter felt nervous excitement as he finally left for Kandep in the red Waso landcruiser around 3 o'clock in the afternoon with Timothy at the wheel. Thank goodness the road was better this side of Wapenamanda he thought, as they headed north-west for Wabag. He remembered steep zigzagging roads down to Wapenamanda.

"Gutpela rot long Laiagam?" he asked Timothy.

"Liklik," he replied with a grin.

"Here is good," Dieter went on.

"Yes masta. Bihain em i nogut tru."

It did not take long for Timothy's words to be proved correct. On the other side of Wabag the road deteriorated markedly. Dieter was pleased they had not stopped in Wabag but just kept going. The red truck dodged and dipped as Timothy endeavoured to evade the potholes. It would be treacherous in the dark or if it rained. Dieter had hoped to get to Laiagam tonight but as he saw heavy rain clouds travelling towards them along the side of the valley he knew they would run out of time. There was nothing else for it but to spend another night on the road.

"Mi yet slip long kar," Timothy said. "No gut ol i stilim cargo. You come masta. Haus man." Timothy led the way through the bush along a beaten track to a long low house with a kunai grass roof overhanging rough hewn wooden planks tied together with bark twine.

"Wantoks," Timothy explained as he greeted them by name.

Bending double to get through the doorway it took some time for Dieter's eyes to become accustomed to the dark interior. There was no doubt about it, their building methods here were far more primitive than any house he had been in earlier. A fire pit had been dug into the earth floor. Dieter looked around but there was no chimney. The smoke wafted around the interior and seeped out under the roof wherever it could. Some of the men nodded and smiled a black toothed smile as Timothy introduced Dieter in a language he could not understand. A younger man moved the kaukau round in the red embers of the fire testing to see if they were cooked. He dusted the ash off two and handed one to Dieter and the other to Timothy. Dieter thanked him.

"Kasen bilong mi i stap," Timothy enlightened Dieter. "Bipo em i wok long Surunki. Yu laik kisim manki masta."

"Yes I do. Em i save tok Pisin?"

"Liklik."

Dieter nodded. "He would be good while I settle in. I'll see how he goes."
So it was arranged, before Timothy returned to sleep in the truck, that Akali would accompany them to Kandep.

As the daylight waned and darkness deepened in the men's house Dieter was shown his bed for the night – a sloping wooden platform about one foot off the ground at the head end and only half that at the foot of the bed. It was made to suit the short indigenous men but Dieter's legs dangled over the end, resting on the floor. At least he would be warmer, with the remains of the fire and six other bodies around him to generate heat, than Timothy would be in the truck.

After a fitful night's sleep because of the fleas Dieter was up at break of day. Mist still hung around the valley as Dieter went outside and stretched to straighten out the kinks in his back. The men still slept inside. They would not budge till the sun was up. Dieter sauntered down to wake Timothy who was hunkered down under the tarpaulin on the back of the truck.

"Okay to get going now?" Dieter asked.

"Yes masta. Mi painim Akali!"

Dieter was pleased they had stopped when they did, as he took in the shoddy bridge building and deepening potholes further along the road. Now the truck growled as it climbed the mountain passes along a road with sharp twists and turns. The juices in Dieter's rumbling stomach settled lower with all the jiggling and juggling. He would be relieved to reach Laiagam and hopefully be offered a coffee and something to eat. In the meantime he made do with another smoke.

Eventually the truck began to descend into a wide open plateau in front of them.

"Laiagam!" Timothy stated.

"Good. I need something to eat."

Groups of houses were dotted around the floor below them. Those belonging to the government were noticeable by their sameness wherever Dieter had been. Then there were mission stations – Catholic, Seventh Day Adventist and Apostolic – all saying the same thing with a different accent. What did it matter? Lutheran stations were dotted around in the vicinity of Kandep, Ed had said.

The Waso store was still shut when they pulled up outside. Dieter yawned as he climbed out and stretched his legs.

"Yumi wetim Roland, em i no kamap yet," Dieter said.
When another truck turned up and parked beside them the driver hopped out and approached.
"Hello I am Roland. You must be Dieter," he said holding out his hand in greeting.
"Yes," Dieter replied. "Pleased to meet you."
"Sorry I'm late. I didn't know when to expect you," he apologised.
"That's all right. We tried to get here yesterday but the rain stopped us."
"Yeah, that'd be right," Roland quipped. "You'll get used to it."
Roland showed Timothy and the store boy where he wanted the cargo stacked. Then he got the primus going for a cup of coffee for the travellers and a packet of marie biscuits.
"Sorry there's no toast," Roland grinned. "Don't have the facilities here."
"That's all right," Dieter replied. "I don't have breakfast often. Depends what I'm doing. A cup of coffee and a smoke sets me up."

As soon as possible they were on the road again.
"Kandep, look out! Here we come," Dieter joked. He would be pleased when they arrived with no more driving until he was ready. The next range was higher than the last, over 10,500 feet. The vegetation was more sparse, mainly consisting of low lying bracken and scrub, with very few trees. At the top he asked Timothy to pull over so that he could survey his new domain. The air was thinner and cooler but green valleys abounded lower down with lush vegetation.
"Rot i gut nau masta," Timothy remarked.
"That's good. All down hill."
"Yes masta. Yumi no slip long kar."

At the end of the day when everything was unloaded and Timothy and the house boy had finished their work, Dieter showed them where they could sleep in the bulk store. Dieter liked the way the building had been designed with the bulk store behind the trade store at ground level. The manager's residence perched on top. His accommodation was adequately furnished with an open plan living area, bathroom, office and two bedrooms. The shower was the standard New Guinea variety, a bucket attached to a pulley with a shower rose underneath. A hand pump, (only one manpower) was used to pump water from the rainwater tank to the header tank. After a meal consisting of two cans of Irish stew Dieter sat back on his sofa with a cigarette in his hand and a cup of coffee on the coffee table. He looked out the louvre windows in front of him at the quarry face on the hill not far away. It brought back memories of Lae. I wonder what plants I will find there, he thought to himself. Yes, he would be happy here.

CHAPTER NINETEEN

There was no doubt about it, Dieter's accommodation was much more amenable than what he had experienced in Goroka and Chimbu. In Kandep he had a furnished house to himself with a view out over the airstrip, the government settlement and the countryside around. It did not take long for Dieter to unpack and claim the space, making it his own. He set up the stereo which he could use when the generator was on down in the bulk store. The Sandpipers and Peter, Paul and Mary were his favourites along with his classical selection. He decorated the woven pitpit wall partitions with bird of paradise plumes, arrows and spears. The sunny bedroom he used as an office and slept in the smaller room.

It was a cool morning with clouds still covering quarry hill. A subdued light came through the louvre windows. Twigs crackled in the stove and sparks snapped as Akali opened the door to fuel the fire some more. He filled the kettle from the tap and placed it on top of the firebox to boil. Soon it began to whistle and Akali made the coffee. Dieter stood at the window surveying his domain as he sipped the black sweet coffee.

Sliding his Peter Stuyvesants into his top pocket he went down the stairs on the outside of the building to the store below. Former workers from Lae had followed Dieter to Kandep and he was pleased to have reliable staff. Ed had asked Dieter to find staff that could be trained to take over the roles of store manager and bulk store manager eventually.

FLIGHT TO FREEDOM

"Morning Dieter," Sule greeted him as he walked into the store. Sule was from Madang, of slight build but strong. He spoke very good English as well as pidgin and his own language. Dieter appreciated the way he could oversee others and use his initiative. Marame from Chimbu had arrived with Sule. In the meantime they were sleeping in the bulk store as it was unthinkable that they would find accommodation with the Engas in Kandep. Dieter had already commenced gathering materials to build a compound out the back. Once this was completed Timothy, Marame and Sule could bring their wives to Kandep and live as families again.

The smell of smoky bodies assailed Dieter's nostrils as he entered the store. People were discussing purchases in the Enga language which was foreign to Dieter and he was unable to understand any of it.
"People have bought building materials for the compound," Sule told him. "They're waiting out the back to be paid."
"That's good. Can you look after the stacking of it in the back of the bulk store. I'll go and pay them." Dieter picked up the cash box full of 10 cent pieces, still called shillings. Locals were standing around outside with small tree trunks and branches, pitpit stalks and bundles of kunai grass. He doled out shillings and was rewarded with smiles and nods from those who could not speak pidgin and a 'tenk yu' from those who could. He would need to employ men to weave the matting, help build three houses and dig the huge ditches to drain the swampland.

The noise of a small plane circling overhead interrupted the buying and selling. Dieter popped into the truck and drove across to the airstrip in his role as the postal agent. A TAL Cessna 185 came into view and made the final approach to the airstrip. It bounced on its rear wheel as the plane slowed and the tail dropped to the runway. The blue stripe along the side of the plane was interrupted as the pilot opened the door and jumped to the ground. He ducked under the wing as he approached Dieter. Today Mike was the pilot.
"How are we?" he asked.
"Good thanks," Dieter replied.
"See you've been busy over behind the store. What are you up to?"
"Building a compound for my workers and their families. Got to clear and drain it first. Put barets right around it," Dieter responded.
"Good for you! Any trouble getting the land?"

"No, Lloyd organised that for me. It's on land that the Australian government has leased from the native title owners."

"Well let's see what we've got for you today," Mike went on. He dragged mailbags and boxes of groceries and other supplies from the plane. Dieter gave a much lighter mailbag to Mike to take back to Mount Hagen. Mainly letters for home and family from the European populace and orders for more supplies. The plane came in only once a week unless the weather was bad. Then they would have to wait until another flight could be fitted in. Today Mike was in a hurry as the weather to the north looked threatening.

"I'll be on my way but I'll check on your compound on my flight in next week. Keep up the progress."

"See you next week." Dieter took the mail and supplies back to the store to sort into the various bags. Mail day was a big occasion and soon he would hear motorbikes, jeeps and land cruisers heading his way. Everyone waited till they heard the plane arrive.

That was how Dieter got to meet people and make friends. Early in the piece Lex had turned up with his two-year-old son Danny sitting in front of him on the Honda bike. He was friendly and they started chatting. The next time he came back he invited Dieter round for a meal. This became a regular occurrence and Dieter enjoyed the company. Mirry, Lex's wife, appreciated the freedom she gained to get the meal ready without having to tend to little people. They had had five children in five years. One was still a baby but the others loved riding on Dieter's back as he crawled up and down the hallway to cries of "faster, faster," as he was whipped along.

"The amazing thing is that you come back for more," Mirry said to Dieter on the second occasion.

At length the compound was finished and the families moved in. The last project had been to build a tall fence around the outside, the height of lengths of pitpit. This was to keep the chooks in. Sule's wife was the carer of the chickens in return for some eggs. Dieter also sent word out that he would like to buy some pigs. Pigs being a sign of a man's wealth, meant that every family had pigs that slept under the same roof as them. It was the woman's job to tend them, even breastfeed a piglet on a rare occasion if it was poorly. Soon Dieter had three pigs – a middle sized one and two younger pigs. He was very proud of his purchase.

FLIGHT TO FREEDOM

"We'll be able to feed them scraps and some sweet potato," he said to Sule and Marame as they admired the pigs.

"They'll dig around for other food too," Marame said.

"You'll be able to buy a bride now," Sule laughed.

"Problem is they're already married around here," Dieter smiled ruefully.

"You'll need more than three pigs to buy a good woman," Marame added.

Now that the compound was finished Dieter got down to the real business of building up the store, getting out and about, selling shares in the company. He was not sure that the Engas really understood what it was all about but those who had earned some money selling pyrethrum daisies to the agricultural officers or didiman seemed to understand the idea of buying part of the store. As for the produce Dieter was supposed to be buying from the locals to ship to Laiagam, the selection was very sparse. Mainly cabbages, a few tomatoes and carrots, potatoes and sweet potatoes aplenty seemed to be all that was available. Possibly that was all that would grow in this mountainous area almost 7000 feet above sea level. There was never enough available at any one time to warrant making a special trip to Laiagam with the produce.

It was a warm sunny day. The mail plane had been. Dieter was selling a tin of mackerel to a dusty skinned bearded man with limited pidgin. He had a rolled up smoke behind his ear and wore the traditional woven loincloth with croton leaves tucked into his belt at the back.

"How mas?" he asked pointing to the product.

"One shilling," Dieter replied.

The man fished a folded leaf pouch out of his bark belt and unwrapped it on the counter. He took out one of his two shillings and handed it to Dieter. He smiled and nodded as Dieter gave him the can of fish. Dieter looked up as a motorbike stopped outside. Lex propped his motorbike on its stand and lifted Danny off the petrol tank.

"Good morning to you," Dieter said.

"Gidday," Lex said with a grin. Dieter tousled Danny's white blonde hair. Danny was a good-looking little boy, dressed in shirt, shorts and roman sandals and smothered in UV cream against the sun's rays on his fair skin.

"So what have you got for us today?" Lex continued.

"There's a parcel there today as well as letters. It looks to me as though it's from Father Christmas."

"Well I'll be blowed. So it is," Lex said with a wink. Danny's eyes opened wide and a big smile lit up his face. They did not see all the decorations in the shops up here in the heart of the Highlands or get to sit on Santa's knee for a photo but he knew what it was all about. His big sister Joy-Joy had been making Christmas decorations as part of her correspondence school lessons.

"Can I have a carton of MaLing duck and one of mackerel too. Better give me a bag of rice while you are at it," Lex said.

"How are you going to get all that on the bike?" Dieter quipped.

"Oh Steve will be round in the jeep later. He's got it on the jack just now."

"Right oh! Or I could bring it round."

"No it's okay. Oh I've been meaning to ask, get into awful trouble if I forgot again. Would you like to come around for Christmas Day?"

"I'd love to," Dieter replied.

"Good that's settled then."

CHAPTER TWENTY

Dieter slept in on Christmas day. He had been up late the night before listening to his music and thinking about his first Christmas in Germany when he was four years old. Although they had just arrived as one family out of the homeless hordes, his Oma had managed to get him a Christmas present. The only one in the family to get one, mind you. A pair of soft brown slippers. He could still feel the love and warmth they represented. But now he was far away from all his family. He wondered if Mutti and the children would even think about him. Christa would! She was married now and had moved to Melbourne.

Dieter stretched as he put his feet on the floor. The house boy had the day off so the wood stove was not lit. A cup of coffee was a must so Dieter pumped some pressure into the primus, put a match to the meths in the shallow trough round the burners and waited till almost all the meths had burned. As he opened the knob the jets of kero caught alight. Dieter moved the kettle from the stove and placed it on top. Taking a rinsed mug from the bench he put a heaped teaspoon of coffee and 3 teaspoons of sugar into it. He thought about the young fellows in Lae. They had joked that was how Dieter liked his women – hot, black and sweet. They used to call the young girls 'brown breasted high titters'. He smiled to himself. One day he would like to settle down and have his own family, he dreamed, but the opportunity had not presented itself. He would like to prove all Mutti's dire predictions to be wrong. Oh well he had made a good start in New Guinea but it would take time. The kettle whistled.

Dieter turned off the primus and poured the water into his mug. While it cooled he had a wash, brushed his teeth and dressed. He grabbed clean shorts and a shirt from the neatly folded pile of washing that Akali had left on the chair. He ran a comb through his close cut hair, done by himself using a comb with a blade in it. Mug in hand he stood gazing out the window as he sipped his first coffee of the day.

The sun shone as Dieter drove round to Sauwi. Excited children popped out the door as he pulled up.

"Look what I got!"

"I got a book."

The four older children clambered around Dieter who dutifully admired their presents.

"Welcome," Mirry beamed from the doorway. "Let Dieter come in and then you can show him everything."

There was no need for horsey rides today. The children had balls, bubble blowers, trucks and cars, books, skipping ropes, puzzles and new clothes.

"Wow! What lucky children." Dieter leaned back in the blue and white bucket chair as the children returned to their playing. Baby Grant sat propped up on pillows in the corner trying to stuff a whole block into his mouth. Lex was setting the table while Mirry dished up the Christmas dinner - a feast compared to their normal fare.

"Wash your hands it's time for dinner."

The children scampered to comply. Mirry set the plates on the table and scooped Grant up to wash his hands and put him in the high chair.

It was a festive occasion with sliced tin ham fanned out on the plates, dried surprise peas, diced carrots and rice for the first course. Two large jugs of tang with ice blocks floating on top stood at each end of the table with glasses and mugs in a row. Warm custard poured over plum pudding, topped with a dollop of tinned cream finished off the meal.

"What a meal! That was delicious," Dieter said.

"Thank you. We got some lovely surprises in our Christmas parcels from home. Peas, pudding, cream and ham," Mirry explained, "not to mention the toys."

Once the two younger children were down for a nap and the others were playing quietly the adults had time for coffee.

"Did you hear from your family for Christmas?" Lex asked Dieter.

"No we don't have much contact now," he replied.

Lex had observed that Dieter never talked about his family. He wondered why. At the end of the afternoon Dieter declined the offer to stay for a light meal.

"I have the compound to check, make sure the chooks and pigs are still there," was his reason.

"Fair enough. But we've been thinking. How about we have a party on New Year's Day too, invite the single fellows from round the district. It gets pretty lonely up here for single people."

So it was arranged, a party New Guinea style on the evening of New Year's Day.

CHAPTER TWENTY-ONE

It was a glorious day. The first of January 1970. Dieter arrived early for the party as Lex had asked him to preach a short sermon for lotu in the late afternoon. The sun shone down. There was no sign of rain today. Dieter was awestruck as Lex led him into the grass church. Inside it was dim and cool. Dieter felt the peace descend upon him as he gazed around. The church design was plain and simple made according to the local customs for a house except much taller. Logs cradled on low stands replaced pews on the well trodden dirt floor.

"I guess you could say it's really down to earth," Lex grinned.

"It's magnificent. There is a quiet beauty here. God's grass cathedral," replied Dieter. He left his Bible and notes on the lectern as they walked out. Lex had suggested showing him round the station.

Outside they stopped as they heard and then saw the teacher from Kurap on her motorbike as she puttered past the hedge and turned into Sauwi. Dieter had met Jean once before outside the store. After she collected the mail she was unable to start her motorbike. She had looked flustered as she tried to kick start it. Dieter went out to help and immediately saw the problem.

"Try now," he said as he bent down and turned on the key.

"Thanks," was all Jean said as the bike roared into life and she disappeared round the corner.

Now here she was again! Dieter nudged Lex with his elbow. "I am going to marry that girl," he said as an aside.

Jean got straight to the point. "Ken needs your help. He is stuck up on the range. The truck's in a ditch. Tried to get you on the 2 o'clock sched but must have just missed you."

"How did you get down?" Lex asked. He knew Jean had gone with them to Laiagam for Christmas.

"Marg and I walked, taking turns carrying the baby."

"All right," Lex said, "better get on my way now." He knew it would take him about two hours each way with the tractor and he had no headlights for in the dark. "Sorry Dieter I'll show you round later."

"Of course. I'll wait around for lotu unless you need some help."

"No we'll be right. The tractor does the work. Jean you go and see Mirry. She will find you a sandwich," he said. "Tell her I'll be back about seven."

The tractor chugged down the road as Jean explained to Mirry what had happened.

"Look at me," she said. "I was so embarrassed to see Dieter there with Lex."

"He wouldn't have noticed," reassured Mirry. "Men don't usually."

Jean was not so sure. Her nose, the most prominent part of her face, was bright red. She could feel it prickling and burning from the exposure to the sun. It had taken Jean and Marg two hours to walk down to Ken and Marg's station. Little Kevin, a solid nine month old baby, had needed a feed and sleep. They had done their best, taking turns carrying him and popping one of Jean's Christmas chocolates into his mouth when he began to wriggle and cry in their arms. It was not a very good solution but they had nothing else. Marg had stopped breast feeding him some time before and they had no clean water. It would have been too risky to take water from a stream. Jean's blouse had been decorated with a mixture of melted chocolate and baby dribble right down the front.

"How about a bath," Mirry suggested, "and I'll find some clean clothes for you. Then you'll be ready for the party tonight."

"Party?" Jean said.

"Yes we have organised a party here, for the single men in Kandep." Mirry raised her eyebrows and smiled. "You can't go back to Kurap yet because Stuart and Gail are still in New Zealand. You will have to stay here until we get someone to keep you company."

Jean knew this made sense. Gail and Stuart's son, not used to all the traffic in New Zealand, had run out onto the road and been hit by a car while they were on furlough. He was severely injured and who knew when they would be back. She realised it was mission policy not to have a single person living alone on an outstation, let alone a single woman. It would be almost a month before school started.

Mirry put the plug in the bath and turned on the cold tap (the only tap).

"I'll leave you to get the hot water while I grab you a towel and some clothes."

An urn sat on the wood stove. Jean put a bucket under its tap and ran the hot water into it, then carried it through to the bath. It was great to have a good soak in a bath. At Kurap Jean had a bucket job on a pulley. It had probably been a year since she last had a bath. She sank down into the warm water up to her chin. Mustn't get her hair wet – she did not have any curlers or enough time to get her hair under control again. It would be good to stay at Sauwi a bit longer. She had taught the same children in Kurap for two years now and would have them for another two before they went to the senior class. So there really was not a lot of preparation to do. Her dog Minny was already here, having been looked after by Mirry and Lex while Jean was away.

"Leave the water in the bath when you've finished. I'll top it up with warm water for the children later," Mirry called.

"Come, Minny," Jean said to the dog as she left the bathroom.

Jean felt much better as she set to and helped Mirry with preparations for the evening. When Lex finally came back he teased her.

"All dollied up for the single men's party, eh? You knew what you were doing coming here today."

"I did not," Jean remonstrated. "I intended to go back to Kurap from Ken and Marg's place. The accident had nothing to do with me." Jean blushed to the roots of her hair to even think that others thought she had arranged it like this.

"Don't listen to him. He's just having you on," Mirry said.

Once the three younger children were bathed, fed and in bed after a story or two, the adults began the party organisation in earnest. Lex chose the reel-to-reel tapes to play on his Akai tape recorder – Tijuana Brass; the Seekers; Peter Paul and Mary. Mirry set up glasses and drinks on the bench with snacks and nibbles on shelves and the tops of speaker boxes around the room. The dining room table had a net across it for table tennis in the meantime. A selection of board games was stacked on a coffee table. When everything was ready Jean ducked outside to the long drop loo behind the house. To her dismay as she came back into the house she realised the guests had arrived in her absence – Lloyd the assistant district commissioner, Jeff the agricultural officer and Dieter from Waso. After Lex's comments earlier it would be near impossible for her to walk into the room without blushing. It was what Jean did well! After talking sternly to pull herself together she opened the door and stepped in. Sure enough, she blushed.

"Help yourself to a drink," Mirry invited.

"Thanks," Lloyd said as he went to pour some lemonade.

Jean was thankful for the diversion and walked over to where Lex and Davie were playing ping-pong.

"I'll play the winner," she said.

Lex was the winner but he handed his bat to Dieter with a wink.

"Here, it's your turn," he said.

"You serve," Dieter said to Jean.

Jean enjoyed table tennis but Dieter was not so keen. It was not a game he had played often when he was growing up. After three games he suggested a game of Wide World.

Mirry and Lex joined in too.

"You partner with Jean," Lex said to Dieter. "That way you can teach her as we go."

It was a great deal of fun as each player chose their own coloured plane, picked up a destination card and took off by rolling the dice and moving along the grid on top of a map of the world. The aim of the game was to reach your destination without another player landing on your square and sending you back to base. The player who collected points by reaching all the assigned destinations and getting to finish first was the winner. Dieter and Jean were a good team, managing to move planes surreptitiously while someone went for some nibbles or out to the toilet. They were surprised that nobody noticed.

Finally it was time for supper which was served on the table tennis table. Tea and coffee with cold drinks if preferred, cakes, biscuits, crackers and cheese.

"Sorry there is no wine or beer," Lex apologised.

Geoff responded with, "That's all right! Had enough for the whole year last night."

As the young men said their thanks and left Jean helped Mirry and Lex to clean up. It had been a good evening, they all agreed.

CHAPTER TWENTY-TWO

It was a cool Saturday morning in Kandep. The mist and low cloud had hung around later than usual. Clad in a warm jumper that had not seen the light of day in Lae, Dieter set off in the truck for Sauwi mission station. Sitting on the seat beside him, wrapped in newspaper, was the most enormous turkey he had ever seen. It was excess stock that had been brought in to Wapenamanda for the American missionaries there. Dieter had been offered it at a bargain price. It was almost defrosted by the time it arrived yesterday.

The only problem was that it was too big to fit in the wood fired oven on his stove or anyone else's for that matter. Dieter had consulted Mirry and Lex about the challenge yesterday. Lex was full of enthusiasm.

"We'll cook it in the ground like the Maoris do back home. Have a hangi."

"Yes that would work," Mirry replied. "We could make the umu pit to order that way."

"Of course. Well that's what we'll do then," Dieter joined in. "I knew you'd find a way round it!"

A log fire was well established at a safe distance from the house when Dieter arrived. Mirry's house boy was in charge of putting more logs on the fire to heat the rocks they had collected. Lex was helping other men to dig the pit.

"Gutpela umu," Lex said.

"No masta em i mumu," the men responded.

"Ah, yumi nogat bulmakau.Bikpela kakaruk i stap. Lukim!"

"Ol i kukim long graun mi kolim mumu."
Lex laughed. "Long ples bilong mi ol i kolim umu."
The men nodded in response, grins on their faces.

Soon it was time to transfer some of the heated rocks into the pit. The turkey, wrapped in an ample supply of pitpit leaves and other green vegetation, was lowered on top. Then came the rest of the rocks. Water was poured over to create steam and quickly sealed with the earth from digging the pit. It would take several hours to cook.

Lex went back to the house. "I'll be off now," he said to Mirry. He was going to Murip to pick up Marg and baby Kevin. On the radio sched this morning Marg had called in to say that Kevin had gastro. Ken was away on patrol at outlying villages so Mirry the nurse suggested Marg and Kevin came to stay for a few days till he was well again. That way if he took a turn for the worse at Kandep they could get a plane in to take him to hospital in Mt Hagen.

"I am just putting a cake in the oven," Mirry said. "Might as well make a party of it."

Several packet cakes had been sent in their Christmas parcels from home. They were great for special occasions.

Later that afternoon the turkey, cooked to perfection, was lifted out of the mumu and taken in to be carved. The table was set and plates, already replete with roast potatoes and pumpkin, waited for the final offering of slices of succulent turkey. Four pairs of eyes watched silently from behind the table against the wall. Grant banged his spoon up and down on the tray of the high chair, Kevin slept in a large cane pram nearby after his bottle of electrolyte.

"Kevin chose the right time for you," Lex joked.

"That's just what I was thinking," Margaret replied.

The table was crowded with four children and five adults seated around. Marg and Mirry sat opposite the children with Lex and Dieter at each end. Jean, still waiting for someone to accompany her back to Kurap, was seated on the corner between Marg and Dieter.

"Well that was a sumptuous meal," Lex said as he leaned back in his chair and patted his stomach.

"Thank you Dieter for providing the turkey," said Mirry.

"You are welcome! I couldn't have cooked it without your help and I wouldn't have had all the trimmings, that's for sure."

At the end of the day when the house boy had finished the dishes and Mirry and Marg had washed sticky faces and hands and put six little people to bed, the adults sat around the stove chatting. Jean sat in a bucket chair knitting a jumper for Ken. She loved knitting and it was something to do during the evening in her little grass house at Kurap. Marg had supplied the wool for matching jumpers for Ken and Kevin. After a final coffee or milo all round, Dieter took his leave.

"Thank you for the good company," he said, "but I'd better be on my way and check the compound."

"Righty oh!" Lex said as he stood to his feet and let Dieter out the front door. They chatted briefly and then Lex came back in and closed the door quietly behind him. Jean packed her knitting away, preparing to go to bed.

"Aren't you going to say good night to Dieter?" Lex said.

Jean stood to her feet, startled by Lex's comment. What did he mean? Dieter was friendly towards her but apart from that he had not made any obvious advances. These thoughts raced through her head as Lex grabbed her by the scruff of the neck and with a hand in the middle of her back propelled her out the front door and she heard the key turn in the lock.

Dieter stood in front of her on the landing, just about to go down the steps. He had been admiring the full moon that shone down on him.

"Well," Dieter said almost as startled as Jean.

She had nowhere to go except forward towards Dieter. Relieved that he would not see her blushing in the half light she walked over to him, not knowing what to say.

"Seeing you are here why don't we do something about it," he stated. With that he put his arm around her. All his efforts had been rewarded and he felt a warm glow inside him. Maybe everything was falling into place. He was surprised that Jean had come out on her own to say good night to him. With that he took her in both arms and kissed her gently on the lips. Jean stood in his embrace thankful that Dieter did not seem to find her forward and brazen.

"Why don't you come around for coffee tomorrow afternoon," Dieter said not wanting to lose the moment.

"That would be nice," Jean replied.

That evening Dieter went home singing. It was as though all the bad experiences since leaving Europe had been cancelled. All his dreams were coming true and a feeling of tender love welled up within him.

CHAPTER TWENTY-THREE

The next day was overcast and it looked as though it might rain. The smell of fresh baked bread mingled with that of a large pot of vegetable soup bubbling on the stove. Over lunch Jean asked if she could use the motorbike that afternoon – fuel was very expensive as drums of it needed to be flown in from Mount Hagen.
"Yes sure," Lex said giving Mirry a wink.
"Dieter invited me over for coffee." Jean felt she should explain.
"That's fine." Mirry patted Jean's hand.

Hopping onto the motorbike Jean realised that she was moving out of her comfort zone. It was very lonely to be a single person in New Guinea even when they had a 'bung' and everyone came in from the outstations. After the laughter and frivolity in the evenings when they retired for the night she could hear the couples chatting through the woven pitpit interior walls. She had often longed for someone with whom to share her thoughts. Up till now it all had to wait till she wrote a letter home to her parents and shared with them what she had been doing. Now that Dieter had made his move she wondered where it would lead. He seemed keen but she had been brought up with the understanding that marriage was a lifetime responsibility. There was no doubt in her mind that she was keen to get to know Dieter better. She would follow her heart in the meantime.

Afternoon coffee was a pleasant occasion. Dieter's living area was neat and tidy Jean noted and he was playing Strauss waltzes on the record player. Jean had never been in the house upstairs above the store, in spite of the fact that her brother John had built it for the mission. Gail and Stuart used to live there before the building was sold to Waso.

"A good view from here," she said as they looked out over the airstrip, down the valley and around to the rugged mountain and quarry.

"Yes I sit in my armchair and think I am Pharaoh as the men wind up and down the track collecting stones for the road into the compound here," Dieter said.

"There are none working today though," commented Jean.

"We finished it last month," Dieter replied. "I'll take you down to look at it later if you like." He was obviously very proud of it so Jean agreed. Although she did not know Dieter very well, she admired his confidence and self assurance, qualities that she did not possess.

Over coffee and marie biscuits Dieter talked about how he planned to build up the business for Waso.

"I need to get out and about to encourage the head men to buy shares in Waso. They are the ones with money and influence. Next week I'll be out most days talking to them. Would you like to come with me?" he said, holding his breath as he waited for Jean's reply.

"Yes I'd enjoy that. I don't venture far off the main road on my motorbike."

The romance continued to flourish. No arrangements had been made yet for Jean to return to her little house at Kurap so she stayed on with Mirry and Lex at Kandep. Neither Dieter nor Jean minded in the least. They made the most of it and spent a great deal of time together.

Whenever Dieter went to the outlying villages in the truck Jean went too. The days were warm and it was hot as they travelled down the dusty roads sitting close together with the windows wound down. It was rare to see another vehicle on the road and overtaking would need to be done slowly and with care to avoid the deep ditches on each side, giving them time to wind up the windows if they happened to meet another traveller. When they stopped at a village Dieter blew the truck's horn and the people nearby called out to others to come. The message was shouted in Enga with all the words seeming to run together. All Jean understood of it was the final word 'ibu-oh-oh.'

"Ibu means come," she explained to Dieter, "and of course the oh – oh sound seems to carry well across long distances."

FLIGHT TO FREEDOM

While they waited Dieter set up his small folding table and arranged packets of vegetable seeds to give to the women. Once the produce was harvested it would be bought by Dieter to provide them with cash.

"It's going to take a long time to establish the scheme," Dieter said. "I don't think Ed and the others at Waso realise the difference in climate up here and the fact that the Europeans have not been here as long as in Wapenamanda, Wabag and Mt Hagen." Dieter was not one to give up easily. He was determined to do his job well and take his responsibilities seriously. Especially now with Jean on the scene.

"Maybe the pyrethrum daisy crop will add to their cash in hand," Jean suggested. She had been involved with that last year when the government had flown plants and agricultural officers in by helicopter to train the people. The schoolchildren had been involved in picking the daisies and setting them out to dry.

Back at Dieter's place later she was asked to cook. This involved Dieter selecting cans out of the cupboard for Jean to heat up! Often Dieter invited Jeannie round for the evening meal. The first time he had asked her advice about where to hang his two new paintings.

"I'm not sure where they look best," he cajoled, not that Jean needed much encouragement by now, although she felt she did not possess much expertise in the matter of hanging works of art.

"I'd love to help," she replied.

When she arrived the meal had been prepared by Dieter with help from Akali.

"Let's eat first so that Akali can do the dishes and go home for the night," Dieter suggested.

Tonight they had MaLing duck on steamed rice and it was a delicious treat that Jean was unable to afford on her income. After dinner and the obligatory cup of coffee Dieter 'tried out' the paintings in different positions against the pitpit wall. Even for Jean it was easy to see which was the best position for each painting. The sunset picture was hung in the lounge where the last rays of the sun would reach it in the evening. The cool forest scene hung in the entrance passage opposite the door.

CHAPTER TWENTY-FOUR

News soon spread around the Kandep area that Dieter had a girlfriend. They had not heard it shouted from the mountaintop and there were no grapes growing in Kandep but word certainly travelled. One day Lee Roy from the Lutheran mission came into the store and got talking to Dieter.
"I hear you've got a young lady in your life. Anna suggested you bring her over for a meal. Would next Saturday evening suit?" he asked.
"That sounds lovely," Dieter responded, "but I'll check with Jean and let you know."
Jean agreed that it would be an enjoyable evening out. Most social engagements were at Mirry and Lex's house so it would be a novelty to go somewhere else. Jean had been teaching Dieter to ride the motorbike so they decided to go on motorbikes. Dressed up to the nines, as much as they could, they set off on a balmy evening for dinner at Anna and Lee Roy's place. They puttered along the road side by side, avoiding potholes. It was impossible to talk above the noise of the engines but they were happy to be going out together.

As they arrived and parked their bikes Jean straightened her pale blue dress trimmed with lace. She had made it herself and she felt good in it – the colour and style suited her she had been told. Dieter took her hand as they walked over to the open door where Lee Roy welcomed them. As they walked in Dieter was surprised to see all the guests that were there. He had imagined it would be like the other meal he had with them, just Leroy, Anna and their children, as well as Edith, a nurse working on the station alongside them. Anna's parents were visiting from the United States. Dave and Mona, from a station up on the side of a mountain, were there with their children too. Jean nodded politely and said hello to each in turn, trying to remember names and blushing with the effort.

In the middle of the room was a large table set with the most exquisite tablecloths and napkins, silver cutlery and fancy plates that looked as though they had been taken out of the china cabinet for the occasion. Jean had never imagined that dining with a missionary family could look like this. Dieter however was not showing any signs of concern. While the small talk went on, Anna and her mother began to bring out dishes full of steaming food and set them on table mats in the centre of the table. There were roast vegetables, glazed carrots, beans and peas, platters of sliced chicken and roast beef, gravy boats brimming with gravy. The table was groaning with food by the time they were invited to sit down. Dieter appeared quite at ease as Jean glanced at him when they sat down. He patted her knee under the table and gave her a smile. After Lee Roy had said 'Thanks' they were told to help themselves.

Jean opened out her serviette and placed it on her lap. Gingerly she began to take a little of this and some of that. It all smelt so delicious and looked so good but she was afraid that she would spill food on the white damask tablecloth. She imagined the horror of a thin line of rich brown gravy sliding off the table and onto her dress for all to see when she stood up.

"Help yourself! Have some more," they urged her as soon as she had successfully eaten everything on her plate.

"Don't be shy! You'll fade away." Lee Roy joked. At last the main course was cleared away, only to be replaced with an array of desserts. Again Jean watched her p's and q's, making sure she used the right cutlery, being careful not to nudge the person on her left as she ate. Jean was the only left-handed person there. 'Cack-handed,' her older brothers used to tease her. She certainly felt cack-handed today. At last after tea and coffee with iced cakes and small talk Dieter felt that they could politely take their leave.

"Thank you so much for inviting us," he said to Lee Roy. "And thank you for the wonderful meal." He nodded to Anna.
"You're welcome," she replied. "Lovely to meet you Jean." Anna smiled.
"Thank you," was all Jean could think to say, pleased that her ordeal was over.

At last they were outside in the cool night air and on their way home. They kick-started the Honda 185s and jumped on to travel back in the dark, their headlights showing the way just a few feet at a time. Dieter led the way in true gentlemanly fashion and Jean came up the rear. He had just rounded the first bend in the road when Jean's motorbike coughed, spluttered and conked out. It had never happened to her before. She tried to start it again but it was no use. There was nothing else for it she would have to walk back, wheeling the bike. As she rounded the bend she could see the tail light on Dieter's bike disappearing in the distance. Jean pushed on until she could not see the tail light at all. She wondered how long it would take her to walk back and when Dieter might realise she was not following any longer. But now a large light was coming towards her. Dieter must have turned around and was coming back.
"What's happened?" he asked as he propped his bike on the stand. "Are you all right?"
"Yes," Jean answered sheepishly. "I think I've run out of petrol."
"Never mind! We'll park the bike on the side and come back in the morning. Jump on behind me."
Jean was not sure how good Dieter's motorbike skills were, he had only learnt yesterday.
"You hop on the back!" she said. "I have been riding motorbikes longer than you."
In the morning Lex took Jean and a can of petrol back to pick up the bike.
"I thought it was the young man who usually ran out of petrol," he said with a grin.

CHAPTER TWENTY-FIVE

By mid January temporary arrangements had been made so that Jean would have company and could return to Kurap for the beginning of the school year. Pauline, a schoolteacher at Laiagam, was to be her companion and take the senior class. Although Kurap was only an hour away from Kandep, Dieter and Jean would not be able to spend so much time together.

"I will come up and see you each Sunday," Dieter suggested.

"Thank you. I'll look forward to it," Jean smiled and gave him a quick peck on the cheek. Dieter was required to work on Saturday mornings and staying overnight at Kurap was not an option. Pauline, a single woman in her late 30s, of strict English stock lived in one house and Jean in her small, single-roomed house with open plan living, including the shower cubicle. A single male staying overnight would be frowned upon.

It was early afternoon by the time Pauline arrived at Kandep and they set off for Kurap in the truck with Minnie on Jean's knee and Lex at the wheel. Mirry had given Jean a loaf of her home-made bread and biscuits to start them off. Bread could be brought in by plane from Wewak once a week but most women made their own so that it would be fresh. At Kurap there was no airstrip so a 'runner' would walk to Kandep to collect supplies. Often they would be caught in the rain and stop overnight in a wantok's house. The low roof with no chimney and an open fire in the middle of the floor where they cooked sweet potato meant that the knapsack with supplies in it could become very smoky. Add in the fact that it was often wet and used as a pillow to cushion the runner's head as he slept on the floor, the bread could well be smoked and squashed. Jean had soon learned to make her own.

When they arrived at Kurap she showed Pauline into the house and explained about the battery charger used to charge the car batteries that powered the lights. Jean went down the pebbled path that led to her house. There was a stale smell in it after being shut up for several weeks. Jean put down her bag and opened the windows, hinged at the top and held open with a stick, then the louvre windows in the living room. It was good to be back but she would miss the family who had lived in the house on the hill. They had formed a close bond over the last two years. Jean looked around her home. At first she had lived in a pitpit two-roomed house with a kunai grass roof. The bedroom was made of permanent materials with flat – iron walls. Now a prefabricated home had been moved from Winja and installed on the precinct. It was more comfortable with no gaps between the floorboards for large hairy moths and other things to wriggle their way through, then circle the light and dive-bomb Jean in the evenings. Usually Jean would cringe in a corner with a rolled up magazine until Minnie could catch them.

All that was in the past now. Jean turned her thoughts to the new year ahead. Pauline would stay for two to three weeks and then Mirry and Lex would move up with their family. And what about Dieter? Their relationship? Jean enjoyed his company and Dieter was attentive. She hoped that the relationship would last now that they were separated by distance. The only communication possible would be by radio – not a smart idea at all, thought Jean, as everyone listened in and added their comments. She would have to wait and see if he visited as promised.

Jean took some kindling from the box beside the stove and laid it on top of scrunched up old magazine paper in the fire box. Once it was alight she added the branches and waited for the fire to draw before shutting the door. Next she filled the kettle from the tap and put it on to boil. An urn stood on the end of the stove. Jean lifted the lid and checked the water level. She'd need hot water later for a shower and washing the dishes. While Jean unpacked the groceries, stacking them in the cupboard, Minnie rearranged her rug on the floor and settled down for a nap. They both agreed it was good to be home. Picking up the receiver on her exquisite old phone Jean gave the handle a couple of turns.

Pauline picked it up on the other end. "Yes?" she queried.

"I'm just putting on a pot of soup in the pressure cooker. Would you like to come down for a meal?" Jean replied.

"That would be wonderful. What time?"

"When you're ready."

Pauline and Jean soon settled into a routine once school started. They had lunch together during the week and sometimes an evening meal as well. Their first job at school was to ascertain how much English the students had retained over the holidays. A teacher boy assisted Jean in the junior class. He had graduated from year six but had not passed the entrance exam to get into high school. There were very few places and only the brightest pupils gained a place. His task was to relay what Jean said to the children in their own language. The system worked well although Jean had caught him out on more than one occasion when he went on to give them the answers. She had a smattering of Enga, enough to alert her. The senior class appeared to be doing well. At first they struggled with Pauline's English accent but they could read and write quite well.

At lunchtime the two teachers strolled up the hill to have lunch at Pauline's house. It was a sunny day but being at almost 8000 feet altitude the air was thin and often cool. When they had prepared their sandwiches they sat down at the table and discussed the morning in class. A cough came from outside the door, followed by two more. This was a signal that there was someone outside who wished to talk to them. Students might wait around outside but they knew not to disturb the teachers unless it was urgent. Jean got up and went to investigate.

At the door was a man with dusty brown skin wearing a bark belt and woven loincloth. His nose was adorned with a pig's tusk that pierced the septum. His tight springy hair was greying. A schoolboy stood beside him looking worried.

"What is wrong?" Jean asked.

"There has been a fight way up behind," the boy said, pointing up the valley in the opposite direction from Kandep. "A man is nearly dead. He has been chopped with an axe." The boy made a chopping motion with his hands, at which point the elder repeated a more violent action.

"So where is the man?" Jean asked.
"He is coming. They are carrying him on a bed."
"All right. So what do you want me to do?"
The boy talked rapidly to the man who responded loudly with arms waving about and eyes filling with tears.
"Can you ask for a truck and the doctor boy to come quickly. He is very sick."
"Our radio time is not till 2 o'clock but I will try another sched. I will get help as soon as I can," Jean said. "But tell the men to keep walking along the road. It will save time and maybe the man's life."
The boy relayed the information and the man nodded. "He said thank you."

Jean turned back inside. She was not sure when the other missions had their scheduled times on the radio. Their own mission sched was at 9 am, 2 pm and 6 pm each day. Often no one except the main station came up at 2 o'clock so she racked her brains. She seemed to remember that Lee Roy's time was around lunchtime. At least she could give it a go she thought, as she plugged the radio in and turned it on. They were in luck, now all she needed was a call sign. Someone called "Delta Yankee. Delta Yankee." Lee Roy answered. Well that was easy. As soon as the conversation was over Jean was in like a shot.

"Delta Yankee this is Sierra Delta. Do you hear me?"
"Sierra Delta, go ahead," Lee Roy answered.
So she was able to get a message through to Lee Roy to be passed on to Lloyd the ADC and the doctor boy at Kandep. It would take an hour for a vehicle to drive up and hopefully the procession bearing the injured man would be past Kurap and nearer to Kandep by then as the road did not continue far beyond Kurap. There was nothing more they could do so Jean and Pauline went back to their classrooms to teach the afternoon session.

Meanwhile at Kandep, Lee Roy had sent the message by word of mouth with his house boy to Lloyd. Lloyd was concerned by the message he got and felt he should let Dieter know before he set off with a polis boy and the doktor boy. As soon as Dieter had set things up for the afternoon at the store he took off for Kurap with Timothy. He was so worried about Jean and Pauline's safety.

"Yu go kwiktaim," Dieter said to his driver.."
"Yes masta, mi save."

The road meandered along the Valley with frequent dips and hollows and many potholes. There were several bridges made of log bearers and smaller logs placed crosswise on top, fastened with bark rope and maybe some bridge spikes securing the logs at each end. Dieter hoped that the girls would be all right. Now they were travelling across a causeway where the road had been built up through swamp. All was fine till they came to the second bridge and the logs moved forward in front of them. Timothy stopped and they got out to survey the bridge.

"Lucky the truck is sitting on the bearers," Dieter said. "But we can't go any further." Now he was feeling really anxious. What should he do?

"Yu go bek isi, isi," he said to Timothy. Dieter stood in front and directed as Timothy put the truck into low ratio and edged it backwards onto firm ground again, but on the wrong side of the bridge. There was nothing else for it, he would have to walk. Leave the truck there with Timothy keeping guard.

"Yu stap long hia," he told Timothy. "Oraitim bris sapos yu ken, na wetim mi."

Dieter took off on foot, to get to Kurap as soon as possible and set the girls free. He suspected that he had left Kandep before Lloyd had a party together. His breath came in gasps as he pushed himself to the edge of his endurance. Not far along the road he met the stretcher party with the wounded man. Dieter looked in horror as they moved a dirty cloth aside to display the man's injuries. He was still alive and had taken an axe blow to his ribs. Dieter watched his lung expand and contract with each breath. Now he was frantic to get there. Finally he rounded the bend and saw the big house sitting atop the hill, still intact as far as Dieter could see. Jean's house nestled at the foot of the hill. But there was no sign of life as Dieter struggled up to the house. All was deathly quiet.

"Jean! Pauline!" He called as he opened the back door. There was no answer. No one was there. Had they been captured or worse?

Then he heard chanting from the school down below the house. Rushing down the path Dieter burst into Jean's classroom. He was red in the face and sweat dripped off him. She had never seen him look so dishevelled.

"What's the matter?" Jean asked.

"Are you all right?" he stammered.

"Yes we're fine. Why?"
"I got such an awful fright! Lloyd told me you were holed up in your house and there was a tribal fight going on. Houses being burned." Dieter stopped for breath.
"What say you go up to the house and have a coffee. It is nearly time to finish for the day. I'll tell Pauline."
Poor Dieter!
He could not understand why they had sent such a message. Over a cup of coffee and some sultana loaf Jean explained what had happened and what she had told Lee Roy.
"We were never in any danger! So we went back to school. What on earth did Lee Roy say to Lloyd?"
"Nothing. He sent a message with a boy," Dieter responded.
"Seems like it was a game of Chinese whispers! I'm sorry you got the wrong message."
"Well I am pleased you are both safe and well but I don't think it is right. You women being away up here on your own!"

CHAPTER TWENTY-SIX

Soon after Dieter's fright things changed at Kurap. Jean wondered whether Pauline was not happy there or was it because Dieter had voiced his concerns. It was immaterial really. Mirry and Lex and the five children moved to Kurap into the big house and Pauline went back to Laiagam. It was good to have the company of a family there again.

A mild sunny Saturday dawned. Jean went about her usual chores, cleaning the small house, while a loaf of bread rose on the edge of the stove. Mirry continued the service that Joy, her sister used to do before she returned to New Zealand, washing Jean's laundry in the generator powered twin tub that Joy left behind. The house boy brought it down and pegged it on Jean's clothesline for her. Whistling to herself as she swept and mopped the floors she thought about Dieter coming to visit this afternoon. A pleasant breeze through the louvre windows played with the cream curtains. Minnie lay stretched outside the door sunning herself. She was off guard duty when Jean was home in the weekends.

Once the cleaning was finished Jean put more wood in the stove and checked the oven temperature. Just right for a double batch of biscuits. That way she would have something for afternoon tea with everyone. While the caramel biscuits baked and the smell wafted on the air she lightly kneaded the bread, shaped it into a loaf and slid it into the baking tin to rise again. By the time two trays of biscuits baked and the fire box was stoked to raise the temperature the bread could go in the oven.

Biscuits cooling on the rack and fresh bread baking. It was time for lunch. She toasted two slices of last week's bread over the fire, spread tinned butter on it, followed by vegemite and slices of cheese. She sat at the small table with her lunch to one side, an old magazine in front of her open at the puzzle page, with pen poised. It was a quiet life at Kurap but she loved teaching her class and always found something to do – knitting for the children, dressmaking, letter writing, or reading, mainly Readers Digest condensed books. Deep in thought with the end of the pen in her mouth she gazed out the window. There had been times before Christmas when for no apparent reason she would burst into tears. She hoped that had passed now. As she was no longer on holiday and did not see Dieter every day she really missed him. She had known him for six enjoyable weeks, four of them spending nearly all their time together. At first she thought he was a Yankee as he had a crew cut and a hint of an American accent. But he was not. The crew cut was the result of having to cut his own hair using a comb with a blade. The accent, well, probably as a result of working with Americans at Waso. He seemed a very pleasant young man and extremely good looking as well. Came out to Australia from Germany with his family when he was a boy. Not that he had much to say about it. But she must not sit here day dreaming all day. She made a cup of tea and tested one of the biscuits. Not bad! Then she changed into her shift with the screen printing on it, a skill she had learnt at Teachers College back in New Zealand. Now to take the rollers out of her hair. Rollers were necessary after she shampooed her hair to keep it under control if it was to sit well. Heaven help her if it got wet in the rain! She brushed her hair and was pleased with her efforts. Taking the tin of freshly baked biscuits she headed up to the other house. There she found a scene of domesticity. The house boy washing lunch dishes, Mirry tidying toys after putting Danny and Grant down for an afternoon nap, Lex busy in the office and the older children playing on their big three wheeled trike outside.

"I've baked these for afternoon tea," Jean said handing Mirry the biscuit tin.

"Good oh. Thanks," Mirry replied.

"Hello." Lex popped his head out of the office.

It was not long before they heard the sound of Dieter's landcruiser grinding up the hill in high ratio avoiding potholes and

FLIGHT TO FREEDOM

runnels where downpours made their way down the orange clay road. At least it was dry today and all the bridges had been intact. He was relieved when Mirry and Lex had moved to Kurap, although he missed their company. Naomi, Davey and Delyse bobbed up and down at the fence as Dieter parked the truck.
"Hello I haven't seen you for a long time," he said as he came through the gate.
"Well you have now," Delyse responded.
"Hello, come in," called Mirry from the back door step as Jean walked out to meet him.
"Just a minute," Dieter grinned, putting an arm around his Jeannie and giving her a quick kiss. That was all he would get away with in public, Jean being so shy.
"Have you had any lunch?" Jean asked.
"No just a coffee. Wanted to get here as fast as I could."
"Well there's vegetable soup and fresh bread here. You really need someone to look after you!" quipped Mirry.
"All right! That would be lovely."
Once he had finished his lunch and popped in to see Lex, Dieter came back to the kitchen.
"I am really tired," he said. "Been having late nights. Would it be all right for me to have a sleep down at your place, where it's quiet?"
"Of course," Jean said as she handed him the key.
"What about some music?" Dieter asked.
"Sure. Help yourself. You know how to turn the record player on don't you?"
"No I've forgotten," he said. "Why don't you come down and put it on for me."
"All right." Jean wondered why he was so insistent but she complied.
They walked with arms round each other, down the stone path. Once inside Jean set about choosing Dieter's favourite record from her sparse collection of LPs and put it on the battery powered record player.
"There you are," she said.
Dieter was sitting on the divan which passed for a sofa and a bed. He patted the place beside him.
"Let's have a talk. Come and sit down."
Aha! Jean thought. He does have something else in mind. But she sat next to him anyway. Dieter took Jean in his arms, without more ado,

looked into her beautiful blue eyes and said, "Jeannie I love you. Please will you marry me?"

What a surprise! Jean had not expected the proposal so soon, yet without hesitation she said "yes."

Now Dieter forgot all about sleep. He had been so nervous and all the dire predictions his mother had made over the years rang in his ears. He had felt that he needed to find out once and for all if his mother had been right. Nothing seemed to matter anymore. His Jeannie had said yes without pausing or showing any doubt. He took Jeannie in his arms, stroking her face, repeating "my Jeannie" over and over. Jean stopped smiling only long enough to whisper endearments in his ears.

"Let's go and tell Mirry and Lex," Dieter said long after the record player had stopped and they chatted about the future together.

"Yes. I wonder what they will say," Jean replied.

"I think they'll be surprised."

"Yes, I was!" Jean added.

Jean and Dieter floated on cloud nine up the hill.

"Where is Lex?" Dieter asked. "We've got something to tell you."

Dieter could not wait for Lex to walk down the hallway for the announcement, "Jeannie and I are engaged!"

There were hugs all round from Mirry as Lex yippeed round the kitchen.

"Congratulations! How wonderful!" they said.

That evening after a celebratory meal of curried rice and bully-beef Dieter travelled back to Kandep. He felt as though the trip home was much smoother than usual. The moon shone and he could see the way ahead right down the bush clad valley. His heart sang and he felt happy and light. The past was forgotten. Life was wonderful once more!

Once home he made himself a coffee. With the mug cradled in both hands he settled into the armchair to dream. Looking back up the valley towards his sweetheart he thought about their future. He would be a faithful husband, true to the example of his grandparents, loving and cherishing Jeannie like Opa had cherished Oma. Around 4 am sleep began to overtake him. Taking his shoes off, he lay down on the sofa looking up the starlit valley as he drifted off to sleep.

CHAPTER TWENTY-SEVEN

It was the end of February. Almost a month had passed since their engagement, seeing Dieter only in the weekends. In spite of being ecstatically happy Jean's tearful bouts persisted, out of the blue. Mirry and Lex had been concerned about it. But now Jean, Mirry and the two youngest children were in the Waso truck. Dieter had collected them to go to Sauwi for their engagement party. Lex had taken Naomi, Davey and Danny on his motorbike. Dieter still had no reply from Jean's father, asking for his blessing on their marriage. Jean reassured Dieter that it was sure to be all right and anyway she was twenty-two years old.
"I want to do the right thing," Dieter said. "I never knew my father and I look forward to sharing yours."
Jean loved him for that. The children chattered in excitement. A party for Dieter and Jean. They were going to get married. The smell of freshly bathed little bodies filled the cab. Shafts of light beamed down as the sun broke through the clouds, promising a fine day.

Dieter drove in silence. He was concerned. Although he looked forward to celebrating their engagement and coming marriage, tomorrow Jeannie was leaving for New Zealand.
"Jean appears to be a trifle depressed," Mirry had explained. "It's nothing to do with you, it was happening before. The mission headquarters in Wellington will pay for her fare as part of the agreement."

"I am happy to pay her fare back," Dieter replied. "But I still haven't heard from her father. What if her parents don't accept me and I never see her again?"

Mirry had patted his shoulder. "I think I know Jean well enough. She will stick to her word. It'll be the best thing for her to have a break with her family then come back to a fresh start with her lover boy."

This had assuaged his worries for a time but in the dead of night they returned to gnaw at his insides.

He looked across at Jeannie, talking animatedly to Mirry about their plans. She seemed to be sincere.

"The first thing I'll do when I get home is go with Mum to buy an engagement ring."

"Don't forget our wedding rings!" Dieter added.

"Of course not. And I'll send yours to you as I promised," she went on.

Dieter planned to wear it on his right hand until their wedding day. "Normally wedding rings are worn on your right hand in Germany," he explained, "but I'll change it to the left on our wedding day. Don't want anyone to think we are not married."

Jean smile. "Then I'll need to choose material for my wedding dress and the bridesmaid and flower girl. After that it's up to Mum to make them."

Pauline was to be the bridesmaid, Delyse the flower girl, with Lloyd as Dieter's best man and Davey as page boy. The men would buy suits and Davey's long trousers in Mt Hagen. The wedding was planned for 30th of May 1970 with Lex as the officiating minister. Lloyd would wear his suit again the following weekend for his own marriage to Moira.

Patting her handbag, Jean went on, "I have got all the measurements in my notebook and the engagement photos." Her parents had not seen any photos yet as they were taken by Ken after the letter had been posted and developed in his blacked out bathroom. Jean and Dieter were delighted with them. Ken had offered to take the wedding photos as well.

The engagement party went very well. Gifts had been sent across from Laiagam where Pauline lived. Included too, were presents from the Waso base at Wapenamanda from Ed and his wife and other staff. Of course there was delicious food with all the women contributing. Chances for a 'bung' did not often present themselves in the Highlands of New Guinea. Besides Mirry, Lex and family and the young couple, the others present were Lloyd and Jeff, Ken, Marg and little Kevin, Edith (the nurse/midwife from the Lutheran mission) as well as Ken and Ruth who were new government teachers in the area. There was music, speeches and laughter as accompaniments to the tempting plates of savouries, pikelets with jam and dollops of tinned cream and chocolate topped slices. An angel cake had pride of place on a plate stand in the middle of the table. It was covered in frosting with peaks all over it. Flowers and leaves encircled it on the edge of the plate. Packet cakes in parcels from home were a boon when it was often difficult to find even an egg. Egg powder was not the same! When someone offered eggs for sale with a smiling face at your door you needed to 'try before you buy'– float them in a bowl of water to see whether they were fresh or had a chicken growing inside or worse.

Too soon the evening ended with those who lived nearby heading home. After a long kiss and cuddle and with a heavy heart Jean went to her accommodation at Ken and Ruth's place, where she would stay again when she returned. Dieter went to his house on top of the store where he tossed and turned in his bed wondering how he would cope with the torment of losing Jeannie for two long months when he had just found her.

The next morning was dull and overcast as Jean looked out her bedroom window. She hoped it would clear for the single-engined Cessna, flown by sight, to find the strip and land. Dear God, let it be. Although she knew that she would miss Dieter dreadfully she did not want to delay the parting day. That would make it worse, especially for Dieter. Final packing done after breakfast, Dieter came round to pick up Jean and her suitcase and go back to the store to await the plane's arrival. There would be little work done by Dieter today, Jean could tell, as he drank copious mugs of strong, black, very sweet coffee in between lighting yet another cigarette. In the midst of talking and cuddling, Jean checked her hand luggage once again – plane tickets – the return journey paid by Dieter, entry permit to get back into New Guinea, photographs to show family and friends, cash for the rings, a paperback to read, plus other paraphernalia she thought she might need on hand for the trip.

At last the low hum of the aircraft could be heard as it approached the ridge then dropped down into the valley and circled the strip as gracefully as an eagle in flight. The landing was smooth, Dieter noted, without too much dipping of wings as the small yellow MAF plane landed and slowed to a halt, its rear wheel making contact with a series of small bumps.

"Good morning," Wally said, unfolding himself from the cockpit and walking round to the rear door. He had brought a load of supplies in from Wewak for the missionary families and would fly Jean back to the Missionary Aviation Fellowship base in Mt Hagen. Dieter and Jean stood quietly, arms around each other as they watched the boys unload the plane and stow mailbags and Jean's suitcase for the next leg of the journey.

"I'll miss you. Please write to me!" Dieter said. He could not believe this was happening to him – Jeannie away for two long months. He knew why it was necessary but his mother's nagging, persistent assassination of him as a person echoed in his head. Soon after they had become engaged he had written a letter to Mutti. On the return address on the flap of the envelope he had written FROM: MR & MRS DIETER KLIER. He smiled for an instant as he remembered her response: "What for you write that? I was very shocked." But now, would her prophecies and curses come true? Dieter shuddered.

"Are you cold, Darling?" Jean asked solicitously.

"No just a nasty thought walked by," he replied.

"I know it will seem such a long time till I'm back. Keep yourself busy and please look after my man till then and Minnie."

"That's it," Wally said as he shut the cargo door. "All aboard."

After a lingering kiss in spite of the onlookers, Dieter helped Jean into the plane and buckled her in.

"See you my Jeannie. Please come back soon."

Lex turned up to collect their supplies as the plane trundled down the runway and lifted off. With a final wave Dieter turned away, hot tears blurring his vision.

Lex put a hand on his shoulder. "She'll be back, you can be sure of that," he consoled.

"I hope so," Dieter replied, "but two months is an eternity."

Lex nodded. They would do their best to keep in touch but it was more difficult now that they had moved to Kurap.

"You are welcome to come up in the weekends. No need to let us know – just turn up."

"Thanks Lex for all you have done for me. You introduced me to Jeannie too."

"It's been good getting to know you Dieter. The children think you're the bee's knees, a box of fluffies in fact."

"A box of fluffies? What on earth does that mean?"

"You are just the best, like a box of fluffy ducks! It's a New Zealand saying."

"Gee thanks. I guess it's a compliment. I've never heard that before," Dieter conceded.

"We are heading off soon, back to Kurap. Come up in the weekend. Stay the night if you like," Lex said as Dieter helped him to load the truck.

"All right. I'll take you up on the offer." Dieter turned away. He needed to get back to work.

It would be two more days before Jeannie arrived home in Dunedin. Probably at least a week before he got a letter from her. Tonight she would stay in Kimininga hostel at Mt Hagen. Tomorrow first thing she flew by DC-3 to Port Moresby on the way to Sydney. There she would be picked up by Ian and Dulcie to stay overnight and taken back to the airport on Thursday morning. Wellington, New Zealand was Jean's next landing. A final debrief with the mission board there before the last leg of her journey where her family awaited. From what Jeannie had said about her family, Dieter realised that she had a stable, loving family. He could not help comparing it with his upbringing in Australia. And what did he have to show for himself at 27 years of age? He had no house, car or bank account, no profession or trade. All this amounted to the fact that he had no security to offer Jeannie. All he had was love. Would that be enough in her parents' opinion?

CHAPTER TWENTY-EIGHT

The following Saturday a lonely lovesick Dieter with Minnie beside him, clambered into the truck as soon as the morning trading finished. He was having difficulty sleeping since Jeannie left. And what had he done about it? Stayed up smoking and having another coffee until he was ready to drop. Consequently he had been tardy in getting up in the mornings. Thank goodness he had well trained staff who could manage till he stumbled his way downstairs each day.

As Dieter drove along the familiar road to Kurap he took little notice of his surroundings. Deep in thought, his mind was on Jeannie alone. She would have arrived in Dunedin two days ago. Tuesday, when he had said goodbye at the airstrip, seemed like an eternity. Did her parents approve of him? Had she bought an engagement ring and their wedding rings? If only a letter came soon to put his mind at ease. But would it put his mind at ease? Would it be a 'no go'? Dear God! He could not take much more of this!

The truck followed the road as it wound along the valley, over the causeway where the valley widened and small streams had conspired to swamp the valley floor. The bridges were intact today. There had been little rain lately and the roads were in good condition. Dieter continued to follow his thoughts, caught up in his own bubble of troubles. The wall was thick and he could not escape.

Rounding the bend the Toyota prepared itself for a stiff climb up the rutted and rivulet-veined clay. Or was it Dieter who changed gear? Maybe it was! By the time they reached the top five faces at varying heights peered over the brush fence. Three were jumping up and down with glee.

"Dieter!" They shouted to their parents indoors.

Mirry came out wiping wet hands on her apron. "Why so it is! Good to see you," she greeted Dieter. "Have you had lunch yet?"

"No," Dieter replied. "Couldn't stand my own company any longer."

"We'll soon fix that," Lex grinned. "Come on in."

The weekend was a balm to Dieter's soul. He had no time to dwell on his misery with five young children delighted to see him, ready to continue the games and rides that were part of his repertoire. On Saturday night he slept well as he dropped exhausted into bed. After dinner on Sunday he headed back to Kandep feeling refreshed and duly scolded by Mirry.

"Look at you! You have got dark bags under your eyes. Imagine what you will look like in two months time, if you keep that up. You will look more like the father of the bride than the groom."

Dieter nodded. "But it's so hard without her."

"You have a duty to Jean to look after yourself. Will we see you next week?"

CHAPTER TWENTY-NINE

Two whole weeks after Jean had left for New Zealand a fat letter arrived for Dieter.
"Be back in a while," Dieter said to Sule. "Got a letter from Jeannie."
"Orait, masta."
Dieter clambered up the stairs on the outside wall of the house two at a time. He rushed to his desk and picked up the letter opener as he slipped into the chair. The long sharp point of the carved knife slit the envelope and Dieter wrestled the letter from its pouch. His wedding ring cocooned in soft layers of tissue paper fell out as he opened the pages. He looked at the date. She had wasted no time posting it. Gradually he began to calm down as he read the letter:

My darling Dieter,
How are you my honey? I arrived home safely yesterday and it was lovely to see the family again.
Today Mum and I went to Stewart Dawson's in town and bought the most beautiful engagement ring. Thank you my darling. I can't stop looking at it as the light dances in a myriad of colours on the diamonds. It has a large diamond set on a leaf pattern with small diamonds beside it. You will have to wait to see it. My wedding ring looks lovely with it but I'm keeping it safely in its box. I hope you like yours – it is exactly the same only wider for a man!
Dad still hasn't received your letter but he sends his regards. Both Mum and Dad are really happy for us. Next week Mum and I are going to buy the material for the dresses and Mum will get started. She's a really good dressmaker and I know she'll do a lovely job. My dress will be white but that's all I'm saying

about it. You'll see it on 30th of May! Pauline's and Delyse's will be primrose I think and matching styles.

Ann has not been well again. At first the doctor thought it was just a bad pregnancy but now after two bouts in hospital on fluids only, they think it may be appendicitis. Hopefully it can be managed till after the baby is born, due in early August.

Well I must close now and get this in the post. Goodness knows how long it will take to reach you. I hope you are well and looking after yourself.

Your sweetheart
Jeannie.

Dieter unwrapped the tissue to reveal a gleaming gold wedding band. It was flat, just as they'd discussed together. He slipped it on to the third finger on his right hand. It would stay there until their wedding day when Jeannie placed it on his left hand according to her custom. In the meantime it would remind him of their love for each other, until he could hold her in his arms again.

CHAPTER THIRTY

A week later Dieter was thinking about going to bed one evening when he heard loud voices coming from the compound. Then he heard a woman's cry through the commotion. Quickly he slipped his feet into shoes by the back door and raced down the stairs. Sule and Timothy had taken the truck to Wapenamanda for supplies, leaving the women and children at home. Suddenly there was a bloodcurdling scream.

In the darkness with a little help from a half moon he saw a man forcing his way into Timothy's house. Now he had grabbed Sule'swife and was trying to have his way. Dieter did not stop to evaluate the situation but rushed forward and grabbed the man by his belt and the scruff of his neck. The element of surprise was in Dieter's favour as the man stood up and he frogmarched him out the door.

"Yu mekim wannem long hia?" Dieter said as he propelled him out of the compound. "Raus! Nau! Yu mekim nogut tru. Yu kam long wanem lain?" All the time Dieter kept him moving. He was shorter than Dieter so it was easy to keep up the momentum. When they had crossed the road outside the compound Dieter gave him an almighty shove and the man stumbled into the ditch full of stinking mud.

"Sapos yu kam bek, mi singautim polis." With that Dieter stalked home. How dare he carry on like that when the men were away. He was shaking with anger as he watched out the window to make sure the humbug was not returning. He doubted that he would after his ignominious mud bath. Once he was sure that the man was not lurking in the darkness he went into the bathroom to wash his hands. Only then did he notice that the gold wedding ring from his right hand was missing. It must have caught on the man's trouser leaves as Dieter threw him out. It was pointless going down to look in the dark with a torch or a lantern. It would have to wait till morning.

First thing next morning Dieter was out searching. But he could not find the ring. He offered a reward to the house boy but no one could find it. Dieter hoped it had not stuck in the man's leaves, rewarding him for his devious escapade but he doubted it. In the end he gave up. He would have to write to Jeannie and get her to send another, maybe slightly smaller.

CHAPTER THIRTY-ONE

True to her promise another letter arrived from Miss Jean Rosie a week later. Jeannie! Dieter's letter would not have arrived yet. But it was heartening to hear that she was making preparations for the wedding. The dressmaking was going well. Decisions had been made and all the materials had been purchased. Mum had already cut out Jean's dress and sewing had begun. Mum had made her own wedding dress, Jean said, and it looked beautiful going by the photos.

"The church ladies are organising a kitchen evening for me later on. Seeing no one will be able to come to our wedding I just might model my wedding dress and let them see it. Of course it will need to be finished first. I have started looking for shoes, as well as a going away outfit and sandals to match. Life is very hectic just now. Yesterday Dad took me for a car ride to one of his favourite spots. It's up on the peninsula. We wound along the top road, up and down hills, with magnificent views of the sea. The southerly winds hammer the trees on this side of the peninsula and they have turned their backs on the sea and look out to the harbour. We parked the car up at the summit and took a walking track down to Sandfly Bay. This is where a colony of yellow-eyed penguins lives and we had hoped to see some. I think we must have been too early and they were still out fishing. One day I'll take you there to see them!"

It was great to hear the news but it was only second best. Dieter wondered what Jeannie would say when she had to buy him another ring.

The weeks went by – slowly for Dieter, more quickly for Jean. All the dressmaking was finished and Jean was delighted with the outcome, according to her letters. She had a photo taken wearing her wedding gown with Mum and Dad in the hallway at home, Dieter's photo placed strategically on the hall table. She would bring it with her when she came back so he would have to wait some more. The kitchen evening had been held with Jean's two school friends acting as bridesmaids when she paraded her dress. They had been given heaps of gifts, so many that Dad was going to pack them all up and send them in a crate by sea. But still his heart ached. He would not rest till he could hold Jeannie in his arms again, to care for her and protect her. 'To have and to hold' the wedding vows said.

On the other hand there was not much Dieter could do to prepare for the wedding. He had flown to Hagen with Lloyd where matching suits and white shirts were purchased. So apart from drinking too much strong black sweet coffee and working during the week, visiting the Cullens in the week end, life was dull for the lovelorn young fellow. Jean had kept her word, writing to Dieter most weeks. Dieter had found it more difficult. Apart from the letter requesting a replacement wedding ring he had found it impossible to settle and put his thoughts on paper. Jean had to make do with the loving thoughts that winged their way across the Tasman Sea.

Propped up with a pile of pillows on her bed in the sun porch Jean prepared to write her final letter before heading back. The weather was cooler now and a feeble sun shone through the windows. As she wrote she could hear Mum preparing lunch in the kitchen. It was a comfortable, reassuring sound but so much had changed for her. She felt excitement and apprehension about their forthcoming marriage. Then there had been the shock about Ann's health.

My dearest Dieter,

This will be my last letter before I return to New Guinea – if I wrote another letter I would probably arrive before it.

It has been a hectic and sad time since I wrote two weeks ago. We have put in our order with the photographer and should get them on Monday. All the dressmaking and shopping has been completed as well. The dresses are hanging in the wardrobe until the day before I leave when they will be tenderly wrapped in heaps of tissue and consigned to their own suitcase. The last thing I need is the stress of having to press my wedding dress with a kerosene iron that shoots out flames like a dragon!

Last letter I told you that Ann was recovering well from her surgery for bowel cancer. Unfortunately things took a turn for the worse just after I posted it. She got an infection in her wound and kept going in to labour. Although the doctors put her on a drip to stop contractions, Mum and Dad were called to the hospital in the middle of the night three times as Ann was so ill. It has been a traumatic time. Finally two days ago the doctors decided that they would not stop the contractions any more. Ann went into labour and a tiny little baby girl was stillborn. At 27 weeks she weighed only one pound one ounce. Ann said she was beautiful with dark hair. She was just too small to survive the birth. Since then Ann seems to be growing stronger but it is early days yet. Of course everyone is feeling very sad at the loss but we are hoping and praying that Ann will recover more quickly now.

Well my dear, Mum has just called me for lunch. My favourite – an egg fried in garlic and butter in the omelette pan, with toast.
I love you! I miss you! See you in two weeks.

God bless
Your loving Jeannie

CHAPTER THIRTY-TWO

It was late autumn in Dunedin on Tuesday 5th of May. The sun was shining through a chill wind but Jean and the family were indoors. There was the rustle of newspaper as Dad and Jean packed the last of the engagement and wedding presents into the crate. As time went on the smell of roast leg of lamb tickled the nostrils, especially when Mum opened the oven door to add potatoes, pumpkin and parsnips, sliding them round the sides of the large pan. The phone rang for the umpteenth time as friends said goodbye and wished Jean well.

Today they would have a traditional family dinner in the middle of the day. Like they always did on Sunday. This afternoon Jean and Mum planned to pack the wedding suitcase with tender care. The other suitcase stood in the hallway waiting for toiletries and other final things to be popped in early tomorrow morning. Dad was driving Jean through to Christchurch in the Bluebird. They would need to be up at the crack of dawn to begin the five hour journey. The plane for Sydney left at 2 pm.

Jean wandered into her room. She would not be able to sleep here when she brought Dieter home to meet her parents. As she looked out the window at Dad's veggie patch she felt mixed emotions. Regret at leaving the family again. Relief that Ann was all right – well sort of. It would take a while for her heart to mend after the loss of her little daughter. Anticipation? Yes. Jean was looking forward to seeing Dieter again after two months. And tiredness on top of it all. So much had been crammed into two months made worse by Ann's health scare. But Jean was pleased that she had been there to support her one and only sister.

On the other side of the ocean Dieter prepared for his trip. He thought the day would never arrive. But here he was, his bag packed and driving to Mount Hagen. He still had an irresistible fear rattling round in his head that he revisited from time to time. Jeannie's frequent letters and the positive signs she gave in them helped to assuage the nasty thoughts. Mirry and Lex had done their darnedest for Dieter too. Finally as he drove towards Mt Hagen he realised that he was feeling more confident that their marriage would take place in three weeks. He hummed to himself as he drove. His favourite hymn – Nearer my God to thee – such was his frame of mind, till at last he sailed in to Mount Hagen. Dieter had arranged to stay at Kimininga Hostel overnight and the next as well with Jeannie. It was a pleasant evening but time seemed to have stopped still as though he was holding his breath.

Next morning he decided to visit Namasu in Mt Hagen as he expected Jeannie's flight to arrive early afternoon. Maybe he could learn something there that would be helpful in Waso, Kandep. Trade store business in the Western Highlands was vastly different from the coast. The Namasu manager, Martin, was a young German fellow and most helpful. His father was a Lutheran missionary of the old school and Martin had spent most of his life in New Guinea. He was knowledgeable about the differences between trading opportunities in Mt Hagen with coffee plantations nearby, and further up in the mountains where the locals were subsistence farmers, producing food for themselves. Dieter kept his eye on his watch. He needed to be back in plenty of time for lunch and then on to Kagamuga Airport to await his beloved.

"It has been good talking with you," Dieter said. "Thank you for your time."

"You are welcome," Martin said. "I talked with Renata my wife. We would like to invite you and Jeannie to stay with us tonight."

"Thank you," Dieter replied. "That would be wonderful."

After lunch Dieter headed for the airport. He spent time with the pilots and staff at the TAL hangar. He knew many of them now as they flew in and out of Kandep with supplies and mail. Even so time seemed to drag as his eyes kept watch for the sight and sound of a plane coming up the Wahgi Valley. The problem was that expected

FLIGHT TO FREEDOM

times of arrival were never accurate. Pilots flew by sight with no radar. First one plane came in, a Fokker Friendship and disgorged its passengers, but not Jeannie.

"She'll be on the next one," he said. More coffee, another smoke and then another until around 3 o'clock another Fokker Friendship arrived with the same result.

Helli the chief pilot for TAL came over to chat with Dieter. "Weather is closing in," he said pointing down the Wahgi Valley. "Won't be any more flights today I reckon."

Dieter turned and looked in the other direction. "It's even worse there," he observed.

"Yeah, best to give up and come back tomorrow," suggested Helli.

As Dieter left to go to the main building his heart was heavy and his feet felt like lead. To his surprise he noticed a handful of other people waiting there. Maybe there will be another flight, he thought. Dear God, just one more with my Jeannie on board! He continued to watch down the Wahgi Valley, wishing, hoping, praying. But the clouds thickened and descended on the mountains. Suddenly there was excited chatter from the others who were pointing in the opposite direction. Dieter followed as they moved out to stand along the fence and wait. Sure enough through even blacker clouds from the north a DC-3 was hopping like an old toad over the mountains. At last it circled overhead and with landing gear down, landed with a thump, bounced and then settled on its undercarriage to stop opposite the terminal.

Dieter's eyes never left the plane as the door opened and the first person emerged. It was his last chance today. Surely she was on this flight. No, no and no. A woman with a young child in her arms waved to friends or family as she negotiated the steps. A man carrying a satchel with a jacket over his arm. With dismay Dieter watched, willing Jeannie to step through the door, but afraid he was going to be disappointed. At last, there she was, his Jeannie, who scanned the huddled group and gave Dieter a wave before concentrating on the steep steps. Dieter could wait no longer! With one hand on top of the security fence he leapt over and rushed to enfold Jeannie in his arms. With tears streaming down his face he said, "I missed you so much. I never want to let you go."

Jean was not comfortable staying with people she did not know. To top it off they were German people with a high standard of living, everything to order and in order. But she appreciated their offer of hospitality. After a fitful night's sleep in a strange bed the morning dawdled in through the shutters. After breakfast they would leave for Wapenamanda and then Kandep. First there was breakfast. She did not feel like eating a thing but felt she should for appearances sake. One weetbix would be more than enough, Jean thought as she reached for the sugar bowl.

"Only one is not enough. You have a long trip," Renata commented in her thick German accent.

Wanting to do the right thing Jean took another. The weetbix stared at her as she poured milk from a blue jug. She picked up the spoon, changed it to her left hand and scooped up a small mouthful. What would they think if she ate nothing? Bravely she put it into her mouth but her stomach revolted. Jean stood up hurriedly and raced for the toilet, afraid she was going to throw up. Now they were certain to think the worst!

Dieter looked on with concern as Jean came back into the dining room once she'd collected herself.

"I am sorry but I can't eat anything just now. It must be all the excitement," she explained with a weak smile.

"No matter," Renata said. "Would you like a cup of tea?"

"That would be lovely thank you."

CHAPTER THIRTY-THREE

Dieter was happy! The sun shone and his heart sang as they drove into Kandep the next day oblivious to the turmoil in Jeannie's heart. "Just very tired," she said in response to his solicitous questioning of the breakfast episode. They dropped Jean's luggage off at Ken and Ruth's place where she would be staying till their wedding and went round to the store together. Dieter needed to check that everything was in order and besides he could not get enough of his darling. He wanted her all to himself after the heart wrenching separation. Then back to partake of one of Ruth's special dinners and an evening playing Mille Borne. There was a lot of fun and laughter until it was time to turn in for an early night.

The second night for Jean was even worse than the one before though she knew her hosts and enjoyed their company. She tossed and turned all night, sleeping an exhausted sleep for what seemed like only minutes, when she woke up and went through it all again. Was she doing the right thing? Did she love Dieter as much as he loved her? That thought struck her as she saw Dieter jump the fence at Kagamuga Airport, ignoring all the 'passengers only' signs to have and to hold his wife to be. Should she call it all off? It would not be too late for Dad to return all the gifts that they'd crated up, would it? Had he despatched the crate yet? And what about the fare that Dieter had paid for her to return to New Guinea? She'd have to pay that back somehow. Get a job with the government school in Kandep? Yes she could do that, but they only employed new teachers at the beginning of the school year. That would mean seven months to wait. What would she do in that time? Where would she stay in the interim. And so it went on, her mind spinning out of control. She thought daybreak would never come. It did, finally, sneak up on her.

It was a dismal morning with mist on the mountains. In spite of her warm bed Jean shivered. She knew what she had to do as she waited for someone to stir in the house. At last she heard Ruth up and about and soon she smelt coffee percolating on the stove in the kitchen. Jean eased her weary bones out of bed and pulled back the curtains to let in the light. Opening her suitcase she took out cotton slacks and a blouse with a jumper to wear over the top. She did not worry about her appearance. Who would after stewing all night?

"Good morning," Ruth said as Jean sidled into the kitchen. "Did you sleep well?"

"Not really. I think I had too much on my mind," she admitted.

"How about a coffee and some breakfast," Ruth continued.

"Coffee would be good. But no breakfast thanks." Jean was not about to repeat yesterday's shemozzle. "I'll go and see Dieter after this," she said wrapping her hands around the warm coffee mug. She hoped Ruth would not start asking questions, panic rising in her belly at the thought of it. Ruth knew better than to pry. Jean looked awful, as though she had not slept a wink.

With stomach churning Jean set off to walk the two hundred yards to Waso. Her shoes crunched the gravel along the road as she walked. She knew Dieter had every right to be hurt and angry with her for stringing him along like this, but she had really thought she was doing the right thing. She had been brought up to understand that marriage was for life. Therefore the time to pull the plug was now, not later. Up the stairs to the door she trudged and knocked timidly. No answer! He must be still asleep. She called his name as she let herself in. No answer again. Dieter's bedroom door was open so she went in. There he was sound asleep, oblivious to the blow Jean was about to deliver.

"Dieter," she said again as she shook his shoulder. "Dieter!" Now he was awake as Jean sat on the edge of the bed. "I have to talk to you," she went on.

"What is it my sweet?"

"I'm sorry but I can't marry you," was all she blurted out before bursting into tears.

"Hush my love," was all Dieter said as he took Jeannie in his arms. "That's all right. We'll talk about it later." He wiped the tears away with his hands. "Hush, hush!" And he rocked her gently in his arms. He too had cold feet while she was away but he had confided in Lex and they talked it through.

"What say I make us both a cup of coffee," he said when her sobs had subsided. As they drank their coffee he suggested a plan. "Would you like to go to Kurap and talk with Mirry? I have to work this morning but I could leave at 12."

Jean nodded. "Yes," she said.

"Well you have a sleep while I get on with my work and I'll see you at 12." Dieter took the rug off the chair and tucked it around her on the sofa. He kissed her cheek, stroked her hair and ran his hand down her cheek and along her jaw line. "See you soon," and he slipped out the door.

Jean heard him walking down the stairs but that was it. She fell into an exhausted sleep and heard nothing more till Dieter returned five hours later. They left straight away and headed up the valley to see Mirry, Lex and the children. When they arrived Dieter took Mirry aside when Jeannie was otherwise engaged and told her she wanted to talk this afternoon. He knew that Mirry was kept busy with five children aged five and under so he wanted her to make time. Over the course of the afternoon Mirry made plenty of opportunities but Jean did not respond. In the end Mirry sidelined Dieter.

"I've given several opportunities for Jeannie to talk," she said, "but she's not taken me up on the offer."

"I'll talk to her," he said. He found Jeannie playing with the children outside. "Aren't you going to talk to Mirry?" he asked.

"No, I'm fine. There is no need to talk with her now. Sorry about that."

Dieter kissed her. "So I'll do after all?"

"Yes."

CHAPTER THIRTY-FOUR

Over in the Waso house in Laiagam Dieter yawned and stretched at the start of his day. Then it hit him, today was his wedding day! He luxuriated in the thought as he rose and went looking for a cup of strong, sweet coffee. He sat by an open window cupping the mug in his hands as he reminisced. The engagement months had been up and down. He loved Jean so much but often his fears had overtaken him. While she was in New Zealand he had been afraid she would not come back. In his letters he had poured out his heart to her and told her how much he missed her. But he had posted only one.

Now today was the wedding! He dressed in his suit bought in Mt Hagen and checked that the best man had the rings. At 9.50 am they walked across to the church. Everyone had been busy decorating the woven matting walls with coloured flowers and leaves threaded into the pit-pit. His eyes scanned the building paper topped with embossed apple green material covering the cracks down the aisle of the dirt floor. That had been Jean's idea and it looked lovely. The little portable organ sounded out *Jesu, joy of man's desiring* as Val tried valiantly to compete with the hole in the wheezing bellows. Light came through under the eaves of the church at the top of the walls. Dieter and Lloyd settled down to wait. The church was full of friends and well-wishers. It was an ecumenical affair embracing people from many cultures and creeds from mission stations all around.

Jean had woken to a bright and sunny day. Although they had a relatively short engagement so much had happened. Jean thought back over the past three months. The day after the engagement party she had flown home to family and friends in Dunedin, New Zealand, buying the rings and preparing for her wedding day. The shock of Ann's surgery and stillborn baby. Then back to Papua New Guinea. In spite of all that happened, looking back today, she knew that she loved Dieter and he loved her. She admired the way he was able to dream. He was kind and gentle and so handsome.

As her bridesmaid fastened her into her wedding gown, made with love by her mother, Jean looked at herself in the mirror. Although she had her photo taken at home with her parents this was the real thing. It was beginning at last – her childhood dream of being 'a plain lady with a baby'. As she smoothed her dress and arranged her train behind she thought to herself, please Dorothy don't be too long. I don't want to keep Dieter waiting. She had been marvelous with everything - organised the catering, arranged the flowers and made Jean's frangipani bouquet. Even the cake was baked and decorated superbly by Dot. Jean knew she would be busy putting the finishing touches to something but she needed her hair done so that she could get to the church on time. Delyse and Pauline stood by too.

Dieter looked at his watch. It was 10.05. Jeannie was 5 minutes late. He glanced around and saw smiles gleaming at him from his national friends. His bride was not here yet. Where was she? Had she changed her mind? Fear fluttered in his gut. He glanced at Lloyd who nodded reassuringly. "They're usually late!" 10.20, then 10.25. Finally there was a hush as Pastor Lex asked the congregation to stand. The organ wheezed into life again with the *Wedding March*. There was his Jeannie dressed like an angel with a train flowing behind her. She looked a little nervous but smiled as she moved down the aisle towards him.

As he waited for the congregation to be seated Lex handed Jean and Dieter an order of service. His hand was visibly shaking Jean noted. Only one other European wedding had been held in Laiagam and that was Lex and Mirry's wedding several years before. It was appropriate that he had agreed to conduct their wedding because he was a good friend to both of them. It seemed as though he was more nervous than the two of them put together. His two children David and Delyse were page boy and flower girl but that was not the problem. Lex took his position of responsibility seriously. He had got to know Dieter well when they invited him to their home for meals. Often he would crawl around the house with a pile of children on his back. Dieter would make a good husband and father, no doubt about it. But there were parts of his life, his background, that seemed to be no man's land. Dieter never talked about his family or his childhood in Germany. It appeared to be all locked in a chest and no one knew the whereabouts of the key.

Lex brought his thoughts back to the present. "We are gathered today before God to witness the marriage of Jean Elaine Rosie to Heinz-Dieter Joachim Klier. Would you please rise to sing the first hymn *O perfect love.*" Dieter and Jean exchanged loving glances, Lex relaxed, Delyse dropped her flowers on the floor and David turned to check with Mirry what he should do about it. The congregation's voices joined in the hymn – a prayer for blessing on Dieter and Jean, that their love would know no end. Then Lex prayed for the bride and groom. But what was he saying?

"......Give them enough tears to keep them tender,
Enough hurts to keep their hands clenched tightly in God's
And enough success to make them sure they walk with God…….."
Doesn't he know that I've had enough hurts and feelings of failure already in my life, thought Dieter? Surely there is no need to pray for more!

The ceremony proceeded and it was time to move on to the exchanging of vows. Dieter placed the wedding ring on Jean's finger. His wife, Mrs Klier, his eyes brimming with emotion. Jean gave Dieter his ring with a smile and a heartfelt promise of fidelity. Finally Mr and Mrs Dieter Klier were presented to the smiling well-wishers as the *Trumpet Voluntary* burst from the poor little organ and the young couple walked down the aisle on the first steps of their journey together.

Outside the sun shone and the cameras clicked as they picked their way down the stony path towards the magnificent feast spread on trestle tables under an overhead sail. A hasty discussion ensued.
"It's very late. Do you think we should have the speeches first?"
"Good idea. The plane is due at twelve." There were telegrams from family and friends in Australia and New Zealand. Jean's Mum and Dad and Dieter's Mutti had not met their new son- and daughter-in-law, but sent their best wishes. Finally the cake was cut and everybody could pay attention to the next task - appreciation of Dorothy's food. There were mountains of sausage rolls, savouries, rice dishes, casseroles, vegetables, cold meats and salads, trifles, cakes,

tropical fruits and tinned cream. Dieter and Jean began to fill their plates. They were certainly hungry after their emotionally charged morning. They sat in their position of honour and began to eat. Was that the plane? The droning became louder as the plane came over the range and circled overhead. There was nothing for it but to rush up the hill and change out of their wedding clothes. Jean clutched her train as she went. Back in the house Pauline unzipped her and she let her dress fall to the floor. Pauline promised to look after it later. Jean reached for her pink crimplene dress and slipped into her sandals. Dieter appeared in casual clothes at the same time and everyone clambered into jeeps to see them on their way. No doubt the guests would attend to the food later.

At the airstrip the little plane was waiting. Officially the airstrip was closed for an upgrade. The runway had been torn up in preparation for a new smoother seal but the pilot had assured them that he could get them airborne safely. Quick handshakes, more photos, hugs and kisses and the odd ribald remark ensued as they clambered aboard.

"Here's the top layer of your cake." Dorothy pressed a parcel into Jean's hands. "You'll need more than love to keep you alive!" Lex shut the door and the Cessna bounced down the runway. Even though it was bumpy they were up in the air at last. Over the ranges they flew, able to see for miles, but intent only on the face of the other. Husband and wife!

CHAPTER THIRTY-FIVE

Dieter and Jean looked out the plane window as its shadow skipped over the mountains on their journey to Lake Kopiago. Rugged rock outcrops stood above the sparse vegetation on the razorback hills. Rivers flowed swiftly in the lush green gorges far below. Kaukau mounds dotted the lower sides of the valley. In no time at all it seemed the Cessna began to descend from their lofty vantage point as Lake Kopiago at 5400 feet altitude came into view. It was a small settlement with a government council office and houses, mission compounds, the lake and airstrip leading to the trade store and kiap's office. The pilot pointed out the Apostolic mission station to the left, surrounded by shade trees with a path leading down to the lake itself. The plane landed gracefully on the strip. Bending over to clamber through the small cabin door, they felt the balmy breeze. Then Dieter understood why Kopiago was referred to as Shangri-la, a mystical harmonious valley. Once they retrieved their bags they set off for the trade store to get basic food supplies for their stay. It was shut – on Saturdays it closed at midday. Never mind they would make do till Monday! Back at the airstrip they loaded their bags in the back of the mini moke that had been left at the airstrip for them. Harold had given them instructions on how to drive it. Setting off for Harold and Pam's house up on the rise, they received friendly waves from the local people. Everything was fine as they sailed along on the flat but as the road began to rise, Dieter changed gear. He missed the gear with a graunch, not being used to the vehicle, then put his foot on the brake, intending to start off again. In their euphoria, he had forgotten the fact that the brakes needed some attention, but soon remembered as the tiny tub rolled slowly backwards and with the camber of the road tipped on a precarious angle into the ditch. It came to rest unceremoniously on its side. It had been a gentle slide and neither of them was hurt so they retrieved their bags and set off on foot. Near the house there were local people chatting together so Dieter, using pidgin and gestures requested help from the men to lift the moke back onto the road. This time he left it in first gear as he ascended to their haven away from the world. Jean asked the helpers if they had any fruit and vegetables that they could buy. The women soon turned up with pineapple, bananas, pawpaw, sweet potatoes, tomatoes, lettuce and cabbage.

"I'm not feeling hungry right now," Dieter said as they stored the fresh food in the kitchen. "Let's leave it for later." He went round the house and closed all the curtains in their love nest to curb the inquisitive habits of the local people, such as noses pressed to the fly screens.

Late afternoon while the sun was still in the sky the young couple woke and decided to stroll down to the lake. The track led down through shoulder high grass, with the path padded smooth by the barefoot neighbours.

"Look at that," Dieter exclaimed as the lake came into view. "How can that be? When we arrived the lake was further over there." He shook his head in amazement.

Two dugout canoes were being poled across the lake. A young lad, with no canoe in sight was fishing from an island in the middle of the lake. The fragrance of frangipani blooms wafted on the breeze as Dieter and Jeannie stood with their arms around each other's waists, taking in the scene. They were in paradise. Two native women came down to the lake so Dieter asked about it. As they explained in their halting pidgin, the young lad pulled up the long pole that was anchoring the island in his fishing spot and proceeded to poll the island across to the shore nearby.

"Olsem wanem?" Dieter pointed to the boy as he secured his 'canoe' at the water's edge. The women laughed and showed them the matted water grasses of the island with roots trailing in the water.

"Moningtaim raunwara i stap long arasait," the meri explained. She made beckoning motions with her hands as she explained how the islands drifted over to where they were standing. "Apinun i go bek, raunwara i stap hia."

Dieter nodded. "We'll come in the morning and have another look," he said to Jeannie. Hand in hand they wandered along the track around the side of the lake and stopped to look back at the mission houses on the slope. The haus lotu (church) stood out with a large cross on it, overlooking the lake. Workers' houses were dotted around below it, surrounded by gardens. Large hibiscus flowers swayed as the breeze picked up. There were gingers, poinsettias, angel trumpets as well as banana trees and palms like betel nut and tapioca. Towards sundown mosquitoes encouraged the young couple to return indoors. They looked through the pantry to supplement the only food they had – wedding cake and fresh fruit and vegetables – to make a meal and turn in for an early night.

Next morning they awoke to birds heralding a new day and exotic perfumes drifting in the open window. As Dieter drew back the curtains he saw that the magical lake had indeed moved to the other side of the valley as the women had predicted. In fact it was the matted grass islands that were moving back and forth. Over breakfast Jean and Dieter talked about their wedding day and how everyone had helped to make it special for them.

"And you know what, now that we are married, I have a father at last," Dieter said with tears in his eyes. "My father left when I was two weeks old and I have not seen him since."

"I don't mind sharing my father," Jean said. "I think you'll get on well together."

After rinsing the dishes they set off for the lake again. Two dugouts were pulled up on the bank. No one was around so they decided to try them out.

"I'll hold it steady while you climb in," Dieter offered.

"It's a bit of a squeeze," Jean laughed as she swivelled sideways in order to get her hips in.

Dieter then climbed in and pushed off. As he tried to sit down he realised what Jean had been talking about. The canoe rocked wildly as he tried to change his position. In the end they decided to abort the exercise as it would have been dangerous if they overturned with their hips wedged in place.

"The native people always stand to pole the canoe don't they?" Dieter said.

"Yes and they are much shorter and slimmer than us," Jean added. There was much laughter as they extricated themselves and waded back to shore, pulling the canoe up onto the bank.

The five short days were spent enjoying each other's company, discussing their hopes and dreams and how they had both come from distant parts of the globe with different cultures and languages and met there in the Highlands of New Guinea. Dieter hoped that maybe his life would improve without his mother's influence from now on. That they would blend their cultures and grow together in their love.

CHAPTER THIRTY-SIX

In the blink of an eye Thursday seemed to appear on the calendar and it was time to return to Kandep, Dieter to his work at Waso, Jean as a homemaker until the beginning of the new school year in 1971 when she might be able to get a teaching position at the territory school. As they circled the airstrip and landed Jean looked at her new home on top of the store, the building her brother had constructed about two years earlier. It had a flat iron exterior for easy maintenance with wooden stairs on the outside of the building, leading from the ground to the house above. She was looking forward to turning the house from a bachelor's abode to a home. As the plane taxied there was Sule with the mailbag, his white teeth showing in a broad grin, along with the usual entourage of sightseers from the store.

"Welcome home masta and missus," he said.

"Thank you Sule. Everything okay at the store?" Dieter asked.

"Yes masta."

Helpers carried the luggage on their shoulders as Dieter and Jean wandered back with Sule. They greeted everyone in the store, workers and locals alike. The women were saying "Ay ya" to Jean and giggling as they bit the back of their hands in a knowing way.

Dieter smiled and said to Sule, "I'll be down soon."

He unlocked the door at the top of the stairs and took Jeannie in his arms as soon as they were inside.

"Welcome home, Mrs Klier."

Jean smiled. As they walked into the living area they could not believe their eyes. The place had been pulled apart and reorganised.

"Who would have done this?" Jean asked in bewilderment.

"Bloody Roland," Dieter replied through gritted teeth.

"But how did he get in?"

"I gave him the key in case he needed to stay over when he came from Laiagam to supervise the boys. I thought I could trust him!"

What shenanigans! The double bed and chest of drawers were set up in the lounge room looking out over the towering mountain that had been eaten away by the quarry. The large round washing tub was planted in front of the stove in the kitchen with a towel draped over it.

"Where is the lounge furniture and the table and chairs?" Dieter asked with mounting despair. This was not how he envisaged the homecoming with his new bride.

The kitchen table had been lifted up and over the wall partitions and sat plonk in the middle of the bathroom with barely room to walk around it. It was set with a bottle of wine, glasses and two chairs to sit on if you could squeeze in.

"How am I going to get that out?"

"Over the top, with the help of the boys," Jean replied. Dieter groaned.

The sofa, armchair and stereo were ensconced in the bedroom. At least these could be manoeuvred along the narrow passage. Jean opened the wardrobe. It was jampacked with everything from the kitchen pantry – pots, pans, cutlery, crockery, canned food, a bag of rice, another of rye flour and all the other sundry items.

"Bloody hell," exclaimed Dieter. "He calls this a joke?"

"But where are our clothes?"

"Probably in the kitchen cupboards."

Sure enough all of their clothes had been rooted out, mixed up and stuffed into the shelves. Jean felt like crying. All her hard work before the wedding. Sorting out, spring cleaning, putting everything back in an orderly fashion so that she could make a meal, knowing what was where. As well as that she had incorporated her own kitchen utensils and belongings into the house. At least their wedding gifts were still in Laiagam to be transported over once they were back.

"Might as well get onto it now," Dieter said. "I'll go and get Sule, Tim and some of the others to help."

Jean hunted through the wardrobe for the important things needed for dinner that evening and breakfast the next day. She left them on the bench, lit the fire in the stove, filled the kettle with water and set it over the firebox. Dieter would need a cup of coffee when he was done. It was such a kerfuffle. With grunting and heaving, sidestepping and manoeuvring the men managed to get all the furniture set up in the right places again. Jean decided to leave all her sorting out for the next day.

"Cup of coffee?" she asked Dieter when it was all done.

"Need you ask? I'd love one!"

Over coffee and wedding cake they discussed the joke. What had seemed a joke to Roland had been hurtful to them. He had gone too far.

"What's for dinner tonight?" Dieter enquired.

"Curried tuna and rice, followed by fresh fruit salad."

"Sounds good. But I don't feel like the wine tonight. I might choke on it!"

Dieter went to work with a will the next day, doing a tally of the cash and stock take for products needed. Only then could he drive to the outlying villages up the range to continue business with them. Although it was a poor area with limited opportunities for anything more than subsistence farming it was hoped that the government's pyrethrum project would help them. Only time would tell!

Jean had put the kitchen and bedroom cupboards to rights again. She started making bread, finding a recipe for rye bread in a very old book that she came across. It was not a success. It did not rise at all though she gave it plenty of opportunity to do so and had never had a flop like that before. In the end she cooked it in the hope that it would rise a little in the oven. It turned out like a brick.

"Never mind. I'll feed it to the pigs," Dieter said. "They'll like it."

They didn't! A week later it was still in the corner of the run untouched, just where Jean had left it. She put half white flour in the next attempt and it was perfect.

Dieter decided that he would give one of his pigs to the workers who had done such a fine job while he was away. It would mean they could celebrate his marriage too.

"The bride price should have been given to my father," Jean said with a wry smile, "and anyway one pig, according to New Guinea custom is insufficient for an educated woman like me." She feigned being insulted at the thought.

"I wouldn't have been able to afford you then. I've only got three pigs, soon to be two," he replied.

"If only I'd thought of it when I was home in New Zealand. I could have had a few pigs delivered to Dad as a joke. Imagine trying to house them in a suburban garden."

Dieter laughed. "But then if he had rejected the pigs the marriage would have been called off or negotiations started all over again. Maybe it wouldn't have been a good idea."

"Don't worry. Dad's always loved a practical joke. He would have worked it out."

CHAPTER THIRTY-SEVEN

The young couple settled into their home, work and marriage. They were very happy and getting to know each other, adjusting to life together when suddenly Dieter's world seemed to implode. It was a cold night which was typical in the highlands at that altitude. But that was not the problem. Jean woke suddenly as Dieter sat bolt upright in bed shivering violently, terrified, in a cold sweat which had drenched the sheets. A nightmare had taken him back to the railway station of a newly bombed town in Germany. People were screaming, yelling, looking for family. Smoke and the stench of burning filled the air. Buildings were demolished and the railway line tortured and twisted so they could travel on it no further.

 A sliver of moonlight slipped between the curtains but it could not dispel the darkness. Jean comforted him as best she could but still he shivered.

"Light the candle," he sobbed. He needed to see her face and be reassured that it was a nightmare and not the reality he had experienced as a young child. He hoped that the candle light would dispel the terror. Jean ran her fingers through his hair as she cuddled him. She had no idea what Dieter had experienced as he talked very little about his past. At last the tremors became less violent.

"Let's change the sheets and then you can get warm again," Jean suggested.

Dieter nodded. What must Jeannie think of him? This had never happened to him before. Why now? The questions filed through his mind, like soldiers on high alert. Back in bed, they cuddled up to get warm again.

"This has never happened before," Dieter said as he recounted some of the horrors.

"Ssh. It's all right now," Jean reassured. After a while she felt him begin to relax. "Shall we go to sleep again now?"

"Yes but please leave the candle lit. I'm afraid I'll see it all again."

Jean got up and moved the candle stand further away from the bed. She realised it was not safe to leave a candle burning while they slept but hoped it would be all right. She was a light sleeper at the best of times. Feeling his pain and trauma she would do anything she could to make him feel better.

"I don't understand what happened to me."

"Neither do I," Jean responded. "But we are in this together."

"Do you still love me?"

"Of course I do. I promised to love you always. Remember?"

The nightmares continued for weeks, sometimes the same scene returning to haunt him several times in the one night. They decided, with no electricity at night, a Tilley lamp would be safer than a candle. The dreams varied but they all had the same theme – tragic scenes viewed by Dieter up until he was four years old as they trudged through war torn Germany looking for a place they could call home, somewhere where they would belong once again. Night after night it occurred. Sometimes there was a gap but then the terror began again. Dieter and Jean talked about it with no one. It was best that way as Dieter was ashamed of it. He could not explain what was happening to him in the darkness of night. With his marriage to Jeannie he wanted to put the past behind him as they built a new life together. But there was no explanation to be found as memories from his subconscious surfaced and refused to be laid to rest. Maybe it was the deep emotional experience of being newly married that had lifted the lid on the happenings of the past, memories that had been buried under subsequent years of additional trauma.

CHAPTER THIRTY-EIGHT

Dieter needed supplies from Wapenamanda and Jean decided to go with him as he would have to stay overnight. It was a cool morning as the truck meandered through the Kandep Valley. The sky was overcast but no rain was imminent. Lowering clouds blocked out the sun in the valley. Jean was seated in the middle of the truck between Tim and Dieter who both smoked as they travelled. Cigarette smoke wafted back into the truck as they exhaled out the window. Jean preferred the smell of Dieter's old spice aftershave in between smokes. They talked as they drove, Dieter and Tim about the store and the possibilities for expansion, Dieter and Jean about their plans for the future. They had been married for three months now.

Rounding a bend as they reached the gorge at Surunki Tim pulled up with a start, then proceeded slowly looking at the landscape. Banana trees, betel nut palms and sugar cane had all been hacked down. Gardens were trampled and houses were burning. Tribal warfare was going on between the Wabag and Wapenamanda tribes. Smoke from the destruction of homes and gardens blacked out the valley as though to hide the shame of it all.
Tim stopped the truck. "Yumi mekim wanem?"
Dieter climbed out of the truck to ask what was going on. A man wielding a heavy stick pushed him aside.
"Skus mi, Masta," he said as he walloped a man with his weapon, then stood Dieter back on his original spot.

FLIGHT TO FREEDOM

Dieter realised that it was useless to try and get any sense from them as they were too intent on payback for a misdemeanour from the other tribe, a fight which could go back and forth for a long time. "I think we will move slowly forward," Dieter said as he got back into the truck. "We can't turn around and go back without running over someone and then we'd be mincemeat too."

"Yes! I'm afraid. It's no good staying here either," Tim added. "I am a Wapenamanda man so I could get clobbered as well."

They wound up the windows and locked the doors as they proceeded with caution. The truck inched forward and the warriors parted just enough to allow them through, then closed ranks behind them. They recognised and respected the red and white Waso truck.

"I wonder how long it takes these people to recover from the wounds they inflict on each other," Dieter thought back to his own life and the scars that still affected him.

"It's a way of life," Tim suggested. "Some get killed and there will be a time of mourning. Then you rebuild and start the garden all over again."

It took an extra two hours to reach their destination. Ed Dickie and the other staff were incredulous to think that they had safely negotiated the war zone.

"Now you are here it's a good chance to talk about what's what," Ed said. Dieter climbed the stairs up to the office, thinking they would be pleased to hear the progress he had made in Kandep and where the business was heading. Once they sat down Ed had little to say but Bradshaw, the marketing manager, delivered a bolt of lightning. Dieter's services as manager in Kandep were no longer required. "There's just not enough money in the area so all development plans will be scratched."

Dieter was speechless. It was done, finished.

"We'll put in a native storekeeper," Bradshaw continued, "who will be supervised on a weekly basis from Laiagam. Down the track we hope to sell the store to the local government council."

Dieter was flabbergasted. He felt angry and hurt. Hadn't he done his best to follow Ed's instructions? In conclusion Ed offered Dieter and Jean a bed overnight.

"You can take the truck through to Hagen tomorrow and look for work there. Shouldn't be hard to find a new job. Try Manton Brothers, Steamships or Burns Philp."

Next morning Tim stayed to work in the Waso warehouse while Dieter and Jean left for Hagen. It gave them plenty of time to discuss their predicament and try to understand what had gone wrong. Dieter was nonplussed. "I've done everything they asked me to and more. Only eight months in the job and I'm out."

"But you've told me before there was a limited amount of cash in the area. And there are two other stores nearby."

"I know. But I thought Waso could do it. So did Ed. That's why he gave me the job. Maybe it was Bradshaw. He's in charge of finances," Dieter continued.

"Maybe," Jean replied. She could see that Dieter was angry and his confidence was shaken. "Something will turn up in Hagen, you'll see."

They drove on in silence for a while deep in thought. Getting married to Jeannie was a new beginning for Dieter but now his hopes had been shattered. First the nightmares, now losing his job. What must Jeannie think of him? He was proving to be a poor choice of husband.

"It's a pity they hadn't done their homework properly before I put all that work in for nothing," Dieter continued.

"Not for nothing, darling. We wouldn't have met otherwise."

CHAPTER THIRTY-NINE

First stop in Mt Hagen was Manton Brothers office on the edge of the township close to the shops. Jean waited in the truck while Dieter went in. She could tell he was nervous and wished him well. Sitting in the truck pondering yesterday's bombshell Jean began to see that the confident man she had married was not so sure of himself after all. It seemed that he had to prove he was a worthwhile person by how hard he worked and the results he produced. She wondered why that was so. Had it come about after the nightmares? Or was there something else? When she had tidied Dieter's office after she had moved into their house he had shown her an old biscuit tin with many receipts for money he had sent home to his mother.
"She'll have to manage with her own money now," he said. "Then we can build our own life, buy a house one day for our family and be able to set ourselves up."
At the time Jean had been surprised. He did not talk about his family much, but then they'd had a whirlwind romance with Jean leaving for New Zealand as soon as they were engaged, returning just three weeks before the wedding.

Jean looked up with a start as Dieter came out, a smile on his face.

"I've got a job. Easy as that," he said.
"Really! That's wonderful Honey."
"Come and see where we are going to live," he continued.
He opened the truck door and helped her down as his boss came out with the keys.
"Darrel, this is my wife Jeannie."
"Pleased to meet you. This is your flat over here." He led them to a doorway in a two storeyed house with only one other building between it and the office. It was built of grey concrete blocks on ground level with weatherboards on the top storey. Inside was a small entrance space with a door leading into the downstairs flat.
"Your flat's up here," Darrel said as he started climbing the stairs.
It was a neat furnished flat, two bedrooms, bathroom, kitchen/dining room and lounge.
"The laundry is downstairs, out through the back door," Darrel said, "with a washing machine."
"It looks good," Jean said. There would be no need for a house boy here, she thought, with a gas stove to cook on and a washing machine downstairs. Free fully furnished accommodation with utilities paid for was the usual standard in New Guinea as it would cost employers too much to fly the workers' cargo in from other places.
"See you in three or four days then," Darrel said as they shook hands.
"Yes, see you then."

So it was back to Wapenamanda, pick up Tim to help with the driving and on to Kandep, getting in late that evening. It was a long day but Dieter was buoyed up by the fact that he had another job. The next day they packed up their personal belongings, said goodbye to everyone on the government station and went to have a final meal with Mirry and Lex. The next morning they left for Mount Hagen with Tim so that he could return the Waso truck to Wapenamanda.

The following day Dieter set off to Hagen Kofi where he was to fill in for the manager while he was on leave in Australia. Jean had plenty to do organising their little home, finding places for all their possessions. Later that afternoon she baked a loaf of bread, prepared vegetables for dinner and put chicken pieces in the oven to bake. When Dieter came in from work the first day Jean could see that everything had gone well. A smile lit up his handsome face as he gave her a kiss.

"How was work?" Jean asked.

"Where is my coffee first, then we sit down and I can tell you all about it."

Jean re-boiled the kettle and poured the water into the coffee mugs on the bench. She took them over to the table. Dieter stirred sugar into his coffee as he began to talk.

"Well, I followed Darrel out to Hagen Kofi in the truck so that I would be able to come home under my own steam later. I am relieving for an Australian worker who is home for a month on leave. Darrel introduced me to Harry the head boy in charge of all the coffee buyers and showed me how to do spot checks as the coffee came in – is it dry, no rocks added to make it weigh heavier, check the cash tin and make sure everything tallies. Harry will take me round to the plantations later. So that's what I'll be doing in the meantime."

"Do you think the sugar is dissolved now?" Jean asked as Dieter continued to stir.

Dieter grinned. "I was concentrating on my day."

"You looked pretty pleased with yourself when you came in."

"Yes," he said. "There's nothing to it, just need to make sure everyone's doing their work in an honest fashion. It is much easier than Waso. I had to set everything up there. Here it's all in place for me. Mind you, it's only for a month and after that I'll be working in the office."

"Will that be difficult for you?"

"I've never done that work before but Mr Malik, the accountant, will teach me. They seem friendly in the office. I'll give it my best. There are plenty of opportunities here in Hagen, even if I do lose my job again." Dieter took Jeannie's hand, lifted it to his lips and kissed it. "I'll look after you well, I promise," he said.

"I know you will," she replied. "Once we are all unpacked I'll go to Burns Philp and see if I can get a job there. Might as well start saving for our house!"

Jean enjoyed her part time work at Burns Philp. She worked mornings only, on weekdays. She enjoyed the company and the ability to earn some money again. They had settled into life in Hagen, been there two months already. Dieter was still having nightmares but not as severe or frequent as before. Often they would go for walks after work, hand in hand, very much in love. One Saturday afternoon they drove to Bayer River. Dieter stopped along the roadside where a meri was selling fruit.

"We'll have to buy some of those," he said pointing to a yellow egg shaped fruit.

"What is it?" Jean asked.

"A pawpaw," he replied. "Haven't had any since I left Lae."

"What are they like?"

"Beautiful. Hard to describe what they taste like because they are unique," he said as he began to barter with the stallholder. "Mi laikim planti," Dieter said. "Hau mas?"

A price was soon agreed on and then Dieter began to load half a dozen of the best pawpaws onto the truck. As they went further down the road there were more opportunities to buy pawpaws, Dieter making sure that they were good quality.

"They are no good if they're overripe," he informed Jeannie. "They taste bitter otherwise."

"Who's going to eat all those?" queried Jean as they the tray of the truck was covered in pawpaws by then.

"We are! Might be able to offload some at the office. I'll tell you what! I'd love some on the way home. Here's my pocket knife. Why don't you sit on the back and peel a pawpaw or two. You can hand pieces to me through the driver's window."

So after a crash course in how to peel pawpaws and get rid of the seeds, that's what they did. Jean was amazed at how much Dieter ate. She was busy all the way home.

The other good thing about Mount Hagen was that there was a Lutheran Church there. Dieter was keen to renew his ties so one Sunday they turned up. The notice board outside stated that it was a congregation of the Missouri synod.

"That's like Dave and Mona's church," Dieter said.

After the service the pastor stood at the door and shook the parishioners' hands on the way out.

"Good morning," he said shaking Dieter's hand, as Dieter introduced himself and wife Jeannie.

"We've just moved from Kandep a couple of months ago, after our wedding," he told the pastor.

"Ah, so you were married there, were you?"

"Yes," Dieter continued, "nearby, in the area."

"I see. And who married you?" he queried.

"Well we had two pastors officiating actually – Pastor Lex and Pastor Wilton. Lex took the wedding ceremony and Wilton gave the address."
"Pastor Lex is Lutheran?" The minister looked over the top of his glasses, waiting for the answer. Dieter and Jean were both feeling quite uncomfortable at this point. Why was he interrogating them like that?
"No he is from Jeannie's mission but Wilton is a Lutheran pastor."
"I see," he repeated himself. "Well on that basis I think it would be best if you worshipped at another church." He smiled a thin smile. "Good day."
Dieter felt angry and humiliated.
"How dare he do that! Well, I won't darken his door again. He was so rude."
After asking around they found a welcoming family of faith in the Mount Hagen Baptist Church and worshipped there.

CHAPTER FORTY

At the end of October Jean had been feeling more tired than usual and she was running to the toilet frequently.
"I'll go and check it out at the doctor," she said to Dieter. "It's possibly a urinary infection."
Dieter looked concerned. "Nothing to worry about I hope."
"I don't think so. Better to check it out though."
Dieter gave her a kiss as he headed off to the office. After the morning at work Jean went to visit the doctor. He listened to what she had to say, then asked for a urine sample to test. He left the room and came back a short while later.
"Well there's no sign of infection," he said, clearing his throat, "but the pregnancy test proved positive. Congratulations. There is nothing more we need to do just now. Come and see me any time if you have any concerns. Otherwise I'll see you in a month's time."
Jean hugged the news to herself as she left the surgery. She was overjoyed and Dieter would be too. They had been married five months now and it could not happen fast enough for Dieter. On the way home she decided to go past Coulter's shop where they sold all manner of merchandise other than groceries or hardware – haberdashery, stationery, books. She was keen to start knitting. The only baby wool they had in stock was a pretty pink. Well she could get something in blue or white later, she thought as she sorted through the baby patterns. She chose one for a crocheted matinee set which would suit the pink wool.

Although it was the beginning of the wet season with frequent showers in the afternoon, today was sunny. Hurrying home she stowed the packet out of sight and began to prepare the evening meal, curried sausages casseroled in the oven. That way she would only have to cook the rice later and the dried peas. She would have the place looking and smelling exciting when Dieter came home to hear the news. Island music was emanating from the flat below, the smell of the casserole oozed from the oven and the sun was streaming through the window as Jean heard Dieter coming up the stairs.

"Hello honey. How was your day?" she asked as she poured their coffees and put them on the table.

"It was good, same as usual. What about you?"

"Excellent," she smiled back. "I went to the doctor. He said it's nothing to worry about. Told me to come back in a month. I am expecting a baby!"

"Say that again!"

"We are having a baby. Due around the 2nd of June."

Tears of joy came to Dieter's eyes as he picked Jeannie up and twirled her around.

"That's wonderful news," he said as they sat down at the table.

"I am sure it will be a boy," Dieter said.

"Do you think so? Why do you say that?"

"I just think it is."

As he sipped his coffee Jean got out the wool and pattern.

"See what I have bought. I want to make something for our baby."

"But it's pink! Why didn't you buy blue wool?"

"Because that was the only baby wool Coulter's had. They will be getting more. I'll buy blue next time!"

After all this time Dieter felt that the chains, with which his mother had bound him, had been broken and she could no longer control his life. At last!

They enjoyed planning and dreaming. Jeannie wrote to her sister in New Zealand, who worked as a Plunket nurse with mothers and young babies, requesting a book about the stages of pregnancy and how to care for herself and their unborn child. Ann posted it back with a book on rearing babies and toddlers as well. Now they could follow the development of their offspring in the womb. A short time later Jean left her work at Burns Philp. She was well and healthy but quite exhausted.

Shortly after Dieter and Jeannie found out about the baby, they had a message sent to them by radio from Mirry and Lex asking if they could all stay with them in Hagen as they awaited the birth of their sixth child.

"It'll be great to see them again!" Dieter said, "although we'll have wall to wall people."

"Yes it will be good. And I'm sure Mirry will have some practical advice for me. She has got so much experience."

A week later Mirry, Lex and the five children drove from Kandep to Mount Hagen in a landcruiser. Jean was amazed that they drove all that way just before the baby was due.

"There were a couple of hospitals along the way if I'd been taken short," Mirry said. "I know what's what by now."

It was an enjoyable time of friendship and reminiscing. Evenings were spent playing board games and cards and the flat was filled with laughter. A day or two after their arrival Mirry went into labour and delivered a healthy little daughter Cheryl Marie. They now had three boys and three girls. Shortly after they returned to Kurap, the way they had come – by road, in and on the land cruiser. Dieter and Jeannie shook their heads as they waved goodbye.

Christmas was celebrated in the flat in Mt Hagen, full of hope and joy. Jean was well and the baby was growing although not fast enough for Dieter. He wished it was more noticeable.

CHAPTER FORTY-ONE

It was late February 1971. Darrel Manton popped into the office just as Dieter was thinking about going home at the end of the day.
"Ah good, you're still here," Darrel said taking off his parka. Rain was beating a tattoo on the corrugated iron roof. "Wanted to have a talk with you."
Dieter looked at Darrel's face, fearful of what it might be about but Darrel looked relaxed. He sat at his desk and beckoned for Dieter to come over.
"We have had plans for quite some time to expand our store operations into Mendi in the Southern Highlands. An architect has drawn up the plans and we're about to apply for a building permit. Would you be interested in becoming the manager there and overseeing the project on the ground?"
Well, Dieter was dumbfounded! He'd been afraid that it was another Waso situation. While he had been learning accounting principles and bookkeeping from Mr Malik, he could not see himself enjoying it long-term.
"I'm certainly interested," he said. "When would this happen?"
"Obviously we have to jump through all the council hoops first but we already have a store in Mendi and we're servicing outlying trade stores from there. There is accommodation on the back of the store. A bit cramped, but if you take up the position we'd ensure that the new house was built by the time the baby arrives. When is Jean due?"
"End of May, beginning of June," Dieter replied.

"Well have a think about it and talk with Jean over the weekend. Let me know on Monday."

"So what do you think?" Dieter said after he had told Jeannie about it.

"It sounds good, doesn't it? Maybe you could have a look at what's there now, in the way of accommodation before you give a final answer."

"Sure. I'll suggest it to Darrel."

When Dieter talked to Darrel on Monday he thought it was a good idea.

"I was going to suggest it," he said.

So Darrel and Dieter visited Mendi, looked over the existing plant and the site for the planned development. In view of the new building and manager's house, Dieter took up the offer.

"It's more than a bit cramped," Dieter told Jeannie. "But Darrel said they'll build our house first, seeing as we only have three months before the baby is due."

They were propped up on the bed in the evening dreaming about their future. Jeannie could see that Dieter was excited.

"I saw the plans for the new building and our house too. It's beautiful, Honey. A residence fit for my lovely wife and little baby."

By the next week they were living in Mendi. The room on the back of the trade store was really nothing more than a store room. However it was fully lined, like a long corridor which widened out at the far end with enough space for a double bed, a chair beside it and hanging space for clothes at the end of the bed. When coming in the door from the trade store there was a kitchen sink (with taps) and an electric cook top on the left. Against the window on the right was a made-to-measure small table and two chairs with just enough room to walk between the table and sink bench. Outside were a toilet, shower and laundry. Boxes of personal effects that did not fit in the 'house' were kept in a shed.

Often Dieter went out and about in the truck during the day, building up business while Jean taught herself to smock, sewed baby clothes and knitted. Pleasurable evenings were spent propped up on pillows on the bed listening to records on the stereo, mainly Strauss waltzes, reading, talking or writing letters home. They were happy and contented.

CHAPTER FORTY-TWO

Dinner was over and the young couple was doing the dishes before settling down in their love nest for the evening, when there was a knock on the one and only exterior door. They looked at each other, perplexed, unsure who would be visiting at that time of night, as Dieter opened the door. It was Wally, the Missionary Aviation Fellowship pilot who lived on the Uniting Church mission station where they went to church on Sunday evenings. Dieter invited him in.
"I got a message for you over the radio schedule this evening. It's not good news I'm afraid," Wally told them. "It's from your brother John. Your father is in hospital and has been diagnosed with an inoperable brain tumour." He paused to let it sink in.
Dieter reached out and held Jeannie close as she burst into tears. Her father was dying, the man who was never sick, always fit and healthy. Dad! Surely not? Wally waited.
"We must go and see him," Dieter said. "I want to meet him."
"That's where I can help," Wally put in. "I am flying to Hagen tomorrow for a meeting, coming back in the afternoon. If you like you can come with me, make all your arrangements and come home again in the evening."
"Thank you. That would be wonderful," Jean said. "I could have a check-up at the doctor as well before I fly. I am seven months now."
That night they clung to each other in disbelief. Dad had not been well, having time off work here and there, but Mum had said in her letter that the doctor had diagnosed sinusitis, nothing to worry about.

Next day they flew to Hagen with Wally. It was a busy day but they managed to get it all done – permission for two weeks compassionate leave from Mantons, arranging finances at the bank, then booking flights from Mendi to Dunedin New Zealand. They would fly back via Wangaratta Australia to meet Dieter's family. Finally Jeannie had a checkup with the doctor, and they sent a telegram home to Mum and one to Sydney to overnight there.

"By rights you shouldn't be flying at seven months," the doctor said. "You're healthy and the baby is strong so I'll give you a letter to use if you need it. You're not showing very much, so I doubt if you will be asked."

By mid afternoon they were back in the air and returning to Mendi, thankful that the weather was fine and everything was in place for them to leave Mendi the next morning. The only thing left to do was to pack their bags. They were exhausted when they fell into bed that night. They had been unable to find Dieter's entry visa in the boxes in the shed, which he would need to get back into New Guinea on the way home. But they decided to call it a night.

"We'll get a replacement when we are in Melbourne," Dieter said. "It's no use worrying about it now."

Jean was up early next morning unable to sleep, anxious to be on the way. She made Dieter coffee to get him going, prepared breakfast and showered. At last they were ready. Jean made a quick dash to the toilet, then they walked down to the airstrip at the bottom of the hill with 30 minutes to spare. Jean was worried and this, along with the advanced pregnancy, caused her to require another trip to the toilet, if you could call it that. It was a small hut sporting a hole in the middle of the dirt floor with no support or railing around it. She locked the door and did her best, under the circumstances, trying not to fall over or wet her sandals as she squatted. She needed to repeat the process once more before they were able to board the plane.

"I hope I make it to Port Moresby with no toilet on the plane. This baby of yours is playing football with my bladder," she said to Dieter.

To her relief it was not a problem. All flights connected and everything went well all the way to Dunedin. Mum and Ann met them at the airport where Jean proudly introduced Dieter. Then they got in the car to go straight to the hospital. The sun shone on the paddocks as they drove but it did nothing to warm Jean's heart.

"I thought Dad was dying on Sunday," Mum told them. "He had a massive seizure and stopped breathing but our friend was there and he acted really fast and took control. Called the ambulance. Up till then the doctor was saying there was not much wrong with him. The hospital confirmed my fears that there was something badly wrong."

"How is he now?" Jean asked.

"He is much better now. They have inserted a shunt to remove the pressure on the brain. But there's nothing else they can do, apart from keeping him comfortable," Ann said.

CHAPTER FORTY-THREE

The hospital atmosphere was what you would expect, artificial light, a sanitised environment and the sound of trolleys, everything working like clockwork. Jean's legs were trembling as she walked into the single room where her Dad was being cared for. He greeted her with a big smile, followed by hugs and kisses. Jean introduced Dieter to Dad. He looked remarkably well Jean thought, just the same apart from looking stary-eyed. Occasionally he would stop in mid sentence and ask about an everyday occurrence that he should remember. This was the man with a brilliant mathematical brain who was also skilled with languages, but medical science could do nothing, Jean kept reminding herself. All that was left to him was a steady decline with the love and support of Mum and the family around him. None of the medical staff were saying anything about his prognosis, how long the tumour would take to kill him. Maybe Dad had been told but he never said anything.

It was a sad way for Dieter to get to know the father that he had longed for. He was thankful that they had been able to make the trip in time. Most of their waking hours were spent at the hospital with Dad, reminiscing about family life, joking sometimes, as Dad tended to do. Dieter often sat in the high armchair in the corner, soaking up as much of him as possible.

"Come and sit on my knee Jeannie," Dieter said as she returned from one of her frequent trips down the corridor. Jean did as he bade her, easing herself down gently. Dieter put his arms around her and drew her back against his chest. He put his hands on her bulging belly.

"That's it! Now I can feel our baby moving," he said.
Dad smiled. Later Mum told them that was what Dad used to do when she was pregnant.
"He liked to see you do that," Mum said.
 The week went too fast. Dad's sister, brother and wife visited from Oamaru. Jean was pleased to see them as they were a close family and she had not seen them for two years. The day before they left Dad asked a friend who was visiting if he would be able to pick Dieter up and take him to visit Dad alone.
"There's always been others here and I haven't had a chance to say what's on my heart," Dad explained.
"Sure, I'd be happy to help," the friend replied.
Dieter was surprised but pleased that he would get to spend time alone with his father in law. Once in the hospital room Dieter leant over the bed to give Dad a gentle hug and a kiss on his cheek. Dad pulled Dieter down onto his chest, held tight, prayed for him and blessed him. Tears ran down Dieter's cheeks as he asked Dieter to look after those Dad held dearest in life. Later Dieter told Jeannie about it, trying to work out exactly what Dad meant. They could only surmise that he was talking about Jean's Mum who had a physical disability all her life, as well as Jean. She had a close relationship with her father, living at home until she was 20 when she left to go to New Guinea.
 That evening Jean was very tearful and distraught knowing that the next day before they boarded the plane she would have to say goodbye to her father and never see him on this earth again. It was the hardest thing she had ever had to do in her life. Dieter comforted Jean and cuddled her.
"We'll come back at Christmas time and bring Dad's grandchild to meet him," he said.
The next morning feeling drained, like death warmed up, Jean said the final farewell to her Dad. They all tried to put on a brave face and Jean managed to hold herself together. Dieter could not believe Dad was dying. He had great faith in the neurosurgeon, the best there is he had been told.
"I'll bring Jeannie and the baby back for Christmas," Dieter said.
Dad smiled and said nothing, holding Jean and Dieter to his heart in a final farewell.

On the plane Jean finally let go and sobbed. Dieter tried to comfort her as the plane taxied down the runway and soared into the blue beyond. Dieter could not face the fact that, having just gained a father for the first time in his living memory, he was soon to lose him.

CHAPTER FORTY-FOUR

Apart from the raw emotional start it was a smooth flight to Melbourne. Dieter's sister Christa was there to meet them. It was lovely for Jean to meet her at last. Dieter often talked about Christa. She had a beautiful smile and an Aussie accent mixed in with a hint of German. It was loud and bright at Tullamarine airport, much busier than Dunedin – planes taxiing and taking off continuously, fuzzy announcements that passengers would find difficult to understand, happy reunions of people from a myriad of countries and the clank of baggage carousels. Once they had their suitcases Christa steered them out to the car park, loaded the bags and drove skilfully through the busy streets to the Australian High Commission. There Dieter explained his predicament, that his entry permit had been lost moving house and it had been an emergency situation which prompted him to leave New Guinea without it. He also cited his wife's advanced pregnancy and showed them the doctor's letter. The official was most helpful and stated he would ensure that a new permit would be in the mail to his mother's address by the next day. That task completed satisfactorily Christa took Dieter and Jean to Spencer Street station to catch the afternoon train to Wangaratta. They had enough time to eat pies and drink a cup of coffee before boarding the train.
"I'll see you next week," Christa said. "We'll have more time and I'll take you to see Ingrid and the boys."
"Thanks Christa," Dieter said as he kissed her goodbye.

Jean felt more relaxed now but extremely tired after the last twenty-four hours.

"Why don't you have a snooze for a while. You need it!" Dieter suggested.

"I think I might," she said as she snuggled up to him.

Both of them managed to have a catnap and then looked out the train window at the passing countryside.

"See those mountains over there," Dieter said, "they are really beautiful. The Warby Ranges."

Jean laughed. "Mountains? I can't see any mountains."

"Well they are a long way back," Dieter conceded.

"They're nothing like the mountains we have in New Zealand, the ones we flew over. I doubt that we'd even call them hills," she added.

"I'll take you to see them one day and you'll see what I mean."

Jean patted his hand. "I'm just teasing. I have to say the weather is warmer than in Dunedin and it's autumn in both places."

As they travelled closer to Wangaratta Dieter said, "I haven't seen Mutti for nearly 4 years. I wonder if she's still angry with me for leaving to go to New Guinea?"

"Maybe she's missed you terribly."

"Maybe she has, but it's probably for the wrong reasons. She wanted my pay."

"But didn't you say she is working now?" Jean asked.

"Yes she is, caring for old people. She didn't do that until I left," he went on.

"Perhaps that has given her more independence, a chance to stand on her own feet. From what you've said she always complained about your stepfather's low wages too."

"Yes you're right."

"I think she'll be pleased to see you."

"She'll be dying to see you my love. Always said bad things about me to any of Christa's girlfriends that came home with her. Said I'd never get a girlfriend, no one would want me," Dieter confided.

"Well you have proved her wrong. There you were in the store in Kandep and I couldn't believe my eyes. Just waiting for you to ask me to marry you." Jean laughed.

"That's not how I remember it. You were scared to talk to me, blushed to the roots of your hair if I even looked at you."

"Don't forget I was a well brought up minister's daughter who was taught to wait for the young man to show his intentions."
Dieter smiled. "I am proud of you."
Soon Dieter noticed that the train was approaching the outskirts of Wangaratta.
"We're almost there. I bet Mutti is waiting for us on the station."
Sure enough there she was as they pulled in. She wrapped her arms around Dieter and gave him a hug when they alighted.
"And how is Jeannie?" She said giving her a hug. "Velcome to Aus-tra-li-a," Mutti said, emphasising each syllable of the country that had adopted her.
"Well, thank you."
Once at home Mutti showed them to their room that had a double bed piled high with a feather quilt.
"I'll just put the kettle on and make you a coffee," she said.
"My," Dieter said. "This is her bedroom and she has vacated it for us."
"That's very kind of her."
"I'll have to ask her about the artefacts, the ones I sent home from Lae. I can't see any around," Dieter remarked.
He broached the subject later but most of them were gone, evidently sold to the highest bidder.
The week with Mutti was so different from their time in Dunedin. Here it was a happy occasion, as Mutti proudly introduced her to family and friends. Jean met Dieter's three younger siblings who were still at school – Veronica, Manfred, and Andrew. Then too, she fussed around Jean, trying to fatten her up.
"You cannot be going to have a baby in two months. You are so small," she worried. "Would you like some cherry plums mit streusel on top?" she asked, when Jean had finished a more than ample helping of goulash.
"When I was expecting Dieter I lay on the sofa and ate a whole bucket of cherries alone." As Mutti chuckled her stomach wobbled. "Dieter was 5 kg. I just wanted cherries so I ate cherries. What would you like?"
"In New Guinea I craved pineapple and cheese sandwiches," Jean admitted.
"With bread?" Mutti asked.

"No, just two slices of pineapple with a thick slice of cheese in the middle."

"Well I never heard of that," she responded.

Mutti continued to fuss around her all week. Dieter enjoyed her cooking too, biscuits, cakes, beautiful meals. He was very relieved though when towards the end of the week he received his entry permit in the mail.

So it was back to Melbourne with Christa, visiting Ingrid and her two sons, Stevie, almost three and Mickey just a baby. Then out to Tullamarine, onto the plane and heading back home.

"I must say Mutti treated me well while I was home," Dieter admitted. "They say absence makes the heart grow fonder. It was either that or the fact that she wanted to impress you," he added with a grin.

CHAPTER FORTY-FIVE

The trip to Port Moresby was long but uneventful as they hopped and skipped from place to place on the 'milk run' after they left Sydney. The further north they went the warmer temperatures became. First they had alighted at Sydney, then Cairns and now Port Moresby where the heat and humidity invaded the plane soon after the doors were opened. It was too hot to do anything so Dieter and Jean decided to sit and wait for the flight to Mendi which was due to leave in about an hour. After buying themselves a snack they sat and chatted. So much had happened in the last two weeks, happy reunions and farewells, one that was heart wrenching. They wondered how Dad and the family in Dunedin were travelling. Maybe a letter would be waiting for them when they arrived in Mendi later today.

"I was a bit annoyed with Mutti," Dieter said, "but I might have known she'd sell my artefacts. She has always been hopeless with money. When I bought the furniture and everything for the house in Wangaratta I put it on layby and paid the installments on pay day before taking the rest home to Mutti. Otherwise they'd still be sleeping on the floor and eating off boxes."

"You're joking!"

"Well maybe I am exaggerating a bit. She was all set up before I left so she shouldn't have needed to sell my stuff," he went on. "I was hoping to sell some of it myself and use the money for a deposit on a house when we settle down."

"You can't do much about it now. We'll see what happens when the time comes."

Finally their flight was announced over the speakers. As they walked across the steaming tarmac to the plane Jean said, "I'll be really pleased when we're home and we can sleep in our own bed again."

"So will I," Dieter concurred.

The Polarus Porter took to the air with ease and circled Port Moresby like a bird before dipping its wings and turning to the north-west. Jean settled back in her seat with a sigh of contentment. Dieter looked out the window watching the landscape receding below, mangrove swamps giving way to rugged mountains, the backbone of New Guinea. The flight would take about one and a half hours, again with no toilet on board. Jean looked around at the other passengers, a mixture of Europeans and some New Guineans. One in particular took her eye as he stretched out along the back seat that went from one side of the plane to the other, preparing to have a sleep. There were no attendants on the plane and it was up to the passengers whether they deemed it necessary to use the seat belts provided. Jean and Dieter had fastened theirs as they were well aware that heavy afternoon rains and winds often swept in without much warning.

About half way into the trip the pilot Peter opened the cockpit door and came into the cabin peering out windows.

"Anyone recognise any landmarks? Can't see much for the cloud cover below," he stated.

Passengers looked from one to the other. No one seemed to know.

"Can you keep your eyes peeled and let me know if you spot something," Peter went on. "Without radar it can be tricky." With that he went back into the cockpit leaving the door open.

No one seemed perturbed. Air travel in New Guinea was often like this – seat of the pants stuff! Dieter kept watch at the window, but now it was hard to see any landscape below. They would be fine as long as the pilot kept the plane at the correct altitude. Dieter glanced up the front to the pilot and Jean followed his gaze. There was a bank of instruments on the pilot's panel and above his head was something that looked like a spade handle hanging down. Through the front windscreen they could see a light patch as though there was a hole in the cloud, or the cloud was clearing. The plane changed direction and headed for the light patch. Suddenly Peter stood up, grabbed the handle and arched his back. He put his full strength into it, pushing it forward with his other hand on the controls. The plane nosed up and tipped wildly on its wing, swinging away from where they had been headed. Dieter and Jean watched horrified as they veered away from a limestone cliff. They had come within inches of death, but now they were under the cloud cover and could see where they were flying. There was a stunned silence in the cabin, broken by a scream as the native man on the back seat was thrown around. He sat on the floor where he he'd been deposited and vomited with fright.

Dieter put his arm around Jeannie, concerned for her safety. "Are you all right?"

"Yes I am fine. Got a fright that's all."

"What about the baby? You might go into labour," he worried.

"It's all right," she persisted. "Did you see the bracken and ferns on the cliff?" she asked in a small voice.

"Yes," he replied, "every detail was etched on my mind in that instant. Thank God we were in a Pilatus Porter or we wouldn't have made it home."

Like a bird of the air the plane could swoop and dive as well as soaring and gliding, Jean thought as the intercom crackled into life.

"We will not make it to Mendi today because of the bad weather," Peter stated. "I've received clearance to divert to Mount Hagen where the airline will put you up in the Hotel. Your trip to Mendi will continue tomorrow by DC-3."

Not one of the passengers complained. Shortly the familiar terrain of Mount Hagen came into view as they passed Mount Giluwe and came in to land. The ground crew opened the door and lowered the steps. The passengers began to exit. Dieter and Jeannie were waiting their turn as Peter began to speak. He was still sitting in the cockpit with his head in his hands.

"There must be an easier way than this to earn a living," he said.

Jeannie took Dieter's arm as she walked down the steps to firm ground. "My legs are shaking," she explained. "I feel as though they won't hold me up."

CHAPTER FORTY-SIX

According to the doctor the baby was due in early June. With no trained doctors, anaesthetist or a maternity ward at Mendi hospital it was recommended in such circumstances throughout New Guinea that European women flew out to stay near a hospital two weeks before the expected time of arrival. Jean, in her wisdom and possibly naivety, decided that she would fly out just one week before her due date. She would stay in Manton's flat in Hagen which was still vacant.

The night before she was booked to fly out to Hagen Jean planned a special meal to celebrate their first wedding anniversary as well. It was a sunny evening but cool as the wind swept along the valley and the sun began to set. A candle on the table had been lit and she served the meal – tinned duck with added vegetables and gravy on rice. Dieter sniffed it appreciatively.

"Mmm! You know what I like."

Jean smiled. There was tinned fruit and custard to follow, another of his favourites. The meal was a quiet affair, both thinking their own thoughts, reflecting back on the past year. When the meal was finished and they had cleaned up they reclined on the bed–cum–sofa. Jean's black suitcase stood against the wall under the window, packed and ready to go in the morning, a stark reminder of their imminent time apart. Dieter was unable to get time off work after the two weeks taken to visit Dad and then Mutti, added to the fact that he had been with Mantons for less than a year. He was worried sick that something might happen to Jeannie and the baby. Jean was apprehensive about flying on her own, the first time since the close call they had coming back from the trip, but she kept it to herself, knowing that Dieter had enough fears of his own.

"I'm really worried," he said taking Jeannie into his arms. "What if something goes wrong and I lose you or the baby?" His voice trembled with emotion.

"We'll be fine," Jean assured him. "The doctor said both of us are in excellent health."

"I lost all the people I loved in the past. Oma died suddenly. Then two years later I was snatched away from Opa and Rudi, Heinz and Liesl. I don't know what I'd do if I lost you. I love you so much. I couldn't live without you." Tears slithered down his cheeks as he gazed at Jeannie. She wiped his tears away with her fingers and stroked his face. "Now we're losing your Dad!"

"Try not to worry," Jeannie consoled him. "Hopefully we'll have enough warning and you can fly in for the birth. We just have to trust God that everything will go well."

The next morning after a tearful farewell, Jeannie left on a DC-3 bound for Hagen. Dieter watched as the plane took off, made a wide circle to gain height, climbed over the mountain range and dropped from sight. He plodded back up the hill to the store and worked there for the rest of the day. As soon as it was closing time and the staff had left, Dieter locked up and went to the hotel bottle store. It had been a long day and he needed something to drown his worries. A bottle of gin would do the trick. Back home, alone, worried sick, he didn't feel like eating. He'd just have a gin first, then maybe a tin of something later. It never happened! Dieter finished the bottle and went to bed when he could no longer stand. A short while later his stomach objected and Dieter shuffled outside where his stomach rejected its contents. Finally he staggered back inside and went to sleep, not waking till the store boys pounded on the door in the morning. Now he had himself to worry about as well as Jeannie and the baby. His head thumped! He'd have a strong coffee for breakfast. Maybe something to eat later in the day.

As soon as he had a shower to freshen up and a coffee or two he went to the post office to call Manton brothers and find out if Jeannie was all right. It was a radiotelephone and echoed badly. Fortunately Mrs Pfeng answered, Mr Malik would not have been so understanding.

"How is she?" he asked. "Has she gone into labour yet?"

"Jeannie popped in this morning and she is just fine. Looks as good as she did yesterday. Don't worry," Mrs Pfeng continued, "we'll let you know as soon as there is any change."
Don't worry! Easier said than done! Dieter couldn't help himself. Four times that day he called the office. At the end of the day Mrs Pfeng called Jeannie to come and talk to him. Maybe that would help.
"No, I haven't had any niggles yet."
"Yes I promise I'll let you know."
By the third day Darrel had had enough.
"For God's sake, come to Hagen and see for yourself. You can work in the office and stop driving us demented.

Dieter did not mind being spoken to like that at all. He went straight to the airstrip and saw Morrie at TAL Mendi.
"Yes I can organise that. It won't take me long to make up a load – government dispatches and so forth for Hagen. I'll take the Cessna 185."
At last they were on their way. The weather was fine with only a smattering of fluffy clouds. Sitting next to Morrie Dieter had a bird's eye view as they climbed over the mountain range and slipped down the other side. All he could think about was Jeannie and the new life she carried inside her. Circling Kagamuga airport he hoped he would not have to wait too long before a vehicle would take him the eight miles into town.

In the meantime Jean was happily ensconced in their former flat next to Manton Bros office. No one had mentioned how often Dieter rang to check on her and how much it had rattled Darrel in particular. So it was a pleasant surprise when she responded to a knock on the door and there he was. It was a tearful encounter but this time they were tears of joy. From then on Dieter stayed in Hagen till after the baby was born. He was working under Mr Malik's tutelage again. Mr Malik humphed around the office looking over the top of his glasses at Dieter while Mrs Pfeng teased him no end. None of this worried Dieter. He could see that Jeannie was well and he was on hand for the birth of their first child. The beginning of his hopes and dreams was being fulfilled at last. In the meantime his fears were pushed to the back of his mind.

After work and in the weekends they often visited friends and were invited out for a meal. The due date had arrived but the baby showed no signs of budging. Dieter decided that a trip out on the

FLIGHT TO FREEDOM

Banz road, notorious for its state of disrepair, might jiggle things along.
"Let's visit Jeff and Barbara," he suggested one Saturday. "The corrugations in the road might get things moving."
Jean smiled. "Nothing will happen until nature decides."
"We'll see." Dieter replied as he headed downstairs to put a bag in the ute. Next moment he called up the stairs. "Come and look at this."
Jean locked up and trundled herself down the stairs.
"We've got no windscreen," Dieter continued. "The buggers have stolen it. Run a knife around the rubber seal and whisked it away."
"Why would they do that?" Jean asked.
"Because there's a shortage of windscreens in Hagen just now. The expected shipment hasn't arrived. Darrel was talking about it yesterday."
"So it's look around and help yourself. What do we do now?"
"Well the weather is fine so why don't we go anyway. The only time we'll get dusty is if we are following too close to another vehicle or there is an oncoming truck. What do you think?"
"Sounds good. Let's go."
They enjoyed the visit with Jeff and Barb, laughing over their plight as they had a cuppa and scones.
"You'd think they'd keep a good supply of screens here in Hagen, especially with the condition of the roads," Dieter commented.
"But occasionally things go awry on the Highlands highway," Geoff added. "Or there's problems in Lae."

On the way home Jean and Dieter were chatting. Life was pleasant in each other's company without any pressures. Dieter was trying to find the best potholes and the most corrugations as they wound along the Wahgi Valley. They were travelling slowly as he thought it unadvisable to damage the vehicle or they might have to walk the rest of the way.
"It looks dark up ahead," Jean said.
"Yes but it's a way off yet." Dieter looked up from the road to survey the sky. "We should make it home."
But it was not to be. The clouds rolled in and just as they reached the outskirts of Hagen township they dumped their contents on top of the ute. Jean gasped as the cold water drenched her cotton dress, which clung to her belly, outlining the curves.

"Just a minute," Dieter said turning on the window wipers. "That might help a bit."

Jean laughed. "It's too late now, a few more drops won't matter."

They carried on home. It was useless to stop and get more water in the ute and over them. They laughed as they sloshed upstairs and changed into dry clothes. Neither the bumpy roads nor the sudden drenching had done anything to change the baby's mind. It wasn't time yet!

Jean had been in Hagen for more than two weeks before there were any positive signs of the imminent arrival. A trip to the doctor confirmed her thoughts and he advised that she would need to be admitted to hospital and stay in a sterile environment until the birth. Thank goodness Dieter was on hand, she thought, or his worries would have skyrocketed. They had talked much about the birth and decided that Dieter should be present. Jean could only imagine what a wreck he would be if he paced the corridors outside, imagining what was happening behind closed doors.

There were just four beds in the maternity ward and all were taken when Jean arrived. So it was necessary for her to stay in the general ward across the corridor. There she filled in her time playing Ludo and other board games with a 10-year-old girl who had a bad break in her upper arm which was proving difficult to set even after two attempts under general anaesthetic. Her family lived out of town and could visit in the afternoons only. As Jean was not in labour yet she tried to take the girl's mind off the nausea and pain following each unsuccessful surgery.

"Excuse me for asking," the mother asked Jean, "but what is wrong with you? You seem perfectly healthy, always up and about."

Jean explained that she was waiting for the birth of her first child."

"You can't be!" she exclaimed. "I can't see a thing."

Jean pulled her loose smock back to outline the bump.

"You can't be due yet!" the mother went on. "When are you due?"

"Almost two weeks ago. The maternity ward is full so they put me in here."

She shook her head.

It was Queen's Birthday weekend on the Monday afternoon when things began in earnest. It couldn't have turned out better, with a public holiday for Dieter. The maternity ward was empty so Jean was transferred there.

"So what clothes do you have to dress your baby in?" Sister Francisca asked Jean.

Now the baby was becoming a reality Jean was excited. Was it a boy or a girl? She prayed that it would be strong and healthy with some hair. Floppy babies frightened her. Jean got off the bed and slid her suitcase out from under it. She took out a gown she had made with love and care suitable for a boy or girl, a singlet, nappy and a cuddle rug.

Soon Dr Nadarajah arrived to do an examination. He was the only doctor on duty for both the European wing and the native wing of the hospital.

"So how are we?" he asked.

"Fine," Jean said.

"Not too much pain?"

"No they are about 10 minutes apart."

"Okay. There is pain relief when you need it."

Then Dieter walked in with a concerned look on his face. "How are you sweetie?"

"I'm fine, just getting going."

"That's all right. I'm not going home till the baby arrives."

"That's good," Jean said. "I'm counting on your support."

"Has the doctor been? What did he say?" Dieter wanted to know.

"He was in just a few minutes ago. Said everything is going well but it will be a while yet. He's over in the indigenous ward now. A young lady has been brought in with problems."

Usually they gave birth in the garden, taking a brief spell from their duties, then putting the baby to the breast and burying the placenta before carrying on with the garden. If they were in hospital for the birth then something was wrong.

"He'll pop in from time to time. Anyway Sister Francisca will know when to call him, or the next nurse on afternoon shift."

"As long as you're all right!" Dieter said.

As the pains increased Dr Nadarajah stayed with Jean and advised Dieter how to massage her back and help her breathe through the pains. At last when the baby's head appeared he beckoned Dieter to watch. He motioned to the native nurse who came over with a stainless steel tray to catch the baby as it came out with a whoosh. At 1:10 am on 15 June 1971 Erika Anne had arrived safely and Jeannie was well. After checking her and wrapping the baby Dr Nadarajah handed her to Dieter. Even though his baby, his little girl was pink, purple and blue, covered in membrane and blood Dieter thought she was the most beautiful baby on earth. Jeannie had done this for him. He had seen what she had gone through that afternoon and night. Jeannie watched as tears of joy welled up in his eyes and spilled over his face mask as he thanked God and blessed his little daughter. Shortly after he kissed his two girls goodbye and floated home on cloud nine, a very tired but happy man.

Next morning Dieter woke in a state of euphoria, questioning if he was really a father, did it happen or was he dreaming. When he turned up at the office he had a smile a mile wide.
"Well look at you," Mrs Pfeng said. "What's the news?"
"A little girl born at 1:10 this morning. She's beautiful and Jeannie is fine."
"Congratulations," she replied.
"Well there you are then! Nothing to worry about," Darrel said. "You'll be able to fly back to Mendi this morning."
"I'll need to send a telegram home first and get some supplies," Dieter responded.
"Fine. I'll organise a flight for 11 am. So look sharp."
First he sent a telegram to Mum and Dad in New Zealand. They'd be thrilled to know their first grandchild had arrived safely and Jeannie was well. Then another telegram went to Mutti. As he moved around town getting supplies for himself and the store he met friends from the Baptist Church.
"How's Jeannie?" they asked.
"She's fine," he beamed as he concentrated on making sure he got everything done before returning to Mendi. They did not ask whether the baby had arrived and Dieter in his haste and excitement did not inform them. The only ones in Hagen who knew were his workmates.

On the way out to the airport Darrel talked about the business in Mendi but Dieter had other things on his mind.
"Remember you said we'd have better accommodation down the track?" he said. Darrel nodded assent.
"Well I've been thinking," Dieter continued. "There's no way we can take a new baby home to where we are living, squashed in behind the store. It's unhygienic and totally unsuitable. The new store and

manager's accommodation hasn't been started yet. So what do we do?"
"See what's available in Mendi and get back to me."
"Thanks. I'll do that. Jeannie and the baby will be home in a week or so. I'll have to get moving literally before that."

So Dieter was whisked back to Mendi. The first Jean knew about it was when Dieter phoned her that afternoon. She was the only woman in the maternity ward, none of their friends knew that Erika had arrived and family was far away. Each morning Dieter rang faithfully to check on his girls and Jean struggled to sound bright and cheerful until he hung up. Then she shed a lonely tear or two until it was time to attend to little Erika again. Her heart swelled with love as she nestled the baby in her arms and she nuzzled the breast.

CHAPTER FORTY-SEVEN

Back in Mendi Dieter had been very busy. First he went to see the company that had just completed a two-storey block of flats.
"There are only one-bedroom flats left," the manager said. "The larger ones have been snapped up by families."
"That'll be fine," Dieter said. "My boss is building a new facility which will include living space for us. Can you hold one for me till I get his approval?"
Darrel was hesitant about the cost but Dieter helped him to understand that there was very little housing available for rent in Mendi. Most of it was government owned for government workers. Dieter was delighted when Darrel agreed, completed the paperwork and paid the initial payment. He wasted no time in packing their belongings (much of it still in cartons in the sheds) and transporting it to their new home. The store boys helped to cart it up the steps to their eyrie. In the evenings he did what he could to make the place comfortable. He hung clothes in the wardrobe, towels on the rails in the bathroom and even managed to unpack the kitchen goods and utensils. By 20th June he had run out of time. Tomorrow he was returning to Hagen to pick up Jeannie and Erika.

Looking around the room he was pleased with what he had achieved. It seemed like a palace compared to where they had been. Behind the store there was the constant noise of store boys and customers talking. When it rained the smell of wet bodies crept under the door and the rain beat on the unlined roof. At other times the wind blew dust under the back door and up through the gaps between the floorboards. Two smaller windows were economical as to how much light they allowed into the room and the view outside was depressing – grey sheet metal sheds crowding in, shutting out much of the daylight. Here now bright light shone through the windows during the day and it was peaceful with a view over the valley. The bathroom also served as a laundry with a washing machine fitted snugly in a corner. They had a bedroom separate from the living area, all shiny and new. There was only one more thing Dieter needed to do before he went to bed. Arrange cannas in a vase for Jeannie's homecoming. He filled the jug with water and expertly arranged the tall red lilies and leaves he had picked earlier.

Six days later on 21st June he returned to Hagen on an early flight to collect his wife and beautiful little bundle. The truck was waiting for him to go straight to the hospital. By the time he arrived, Erika had been bathed, dressed in a small gown that Jeannie had sewn and embroidered and finally fed so that they would be ready to go. After kissing Jeannie, Dieter looked down at the sleeping wonder in her arms.

"She's more beautiful than I remember," he said with tears in his eyes.

Jeannie smiled as she handed Erika to him. "Yes," she said. "Would you wrap her in the bunny rug and pop her in the carry basket. Then we can go as soon as I tell the nurse."

Dieter straightened the cuddle rug on the bed and carefully laid Erika in the middle, wrapping it around her. Picking her up, he looked at her tenderly, kissed her forehead then gently laid her in the carry basket, tucking the cover over her.

"Do we have time to get a few things in town?" Jean asked. "It will be good to choose what I want for Erika, rather than rely on an order through the post."

"Yes of course. The plane leaves at one so we can get some lunch as well."

In the town centre the proud parents walked down the main street carrying the white wicker basket between them. Friends and acquaintances stopped to admire the baby and congratulate them.

"She's so tiny."

"What a sweetie."

"I love her name." And so it went on. She was quite small at 5 lbs 11 oz but Jean was proud of the blonde fuzz on the baby's head and her strength to lift her head off the bed when lying on her tummy. Erika was certainly not a bald, floppy baby.

The next stop was Manton Bros office where the staff got to see what all the fuss had been about. Then it was off to the airport and heading to their new home in Mendi. As the DC-3 trundled down the runway Dieter was concerned that the noise might wake the baby.

"She's probably like you," Jean laughed. "Can sleep through a thunderstorm or an earthquake."

They were both deep in thought and cuddled up together as the plane took to the air.

"Most babies go home by car," Jean commented.

"I didn't. I was born at home."

"It's a new chapter in our life now," Jean continued, "having a small defenceless baby to care for. Especially taking her home to a station in New Guinea where there is no clinic where we can get support.

"And no family either," said Dieter. "There are always the nurses at the United Church Mission if we need advice."

"Yes that's true."

It was a daunting prospect for first time parents to come home to an outpost like Mendi with little support.

The flat seemed beautiful to Jean, compared to the room behind the trade store. It wouldn't take long to finish the unpacking once Jean and the baby were settled. Dieter took the rest of the week off work to help Jean as she had developed an infection in her stitches requiring salt baths in a basin (not too full mind) on a kitchen chair. Erika was a perfect baby apart from her restless times in the evenings when Dieter often walked the floor with her over a shoulder, singing, while he put another load of nappies into the washing machine.

One day a visitor arrived unannounced. It was the mother of one of the United Church missionary staff who had flown up from Adelaide on holiday. Grandma Ayling was a godsend! She did ironing, cleaning and cooked a meal, whatever needed doing, for a week. By then Jean was much better and the young parents had begun to know the needs of their little one. They developed a routine and Dieter was able to return to work.

A week after their return from Hagen a letter arrived in the mail, forwarded on by Manton Bros. Dieter had opened it at the store and with a heavy heart he brought it home to Jean. Inside the envelope was a telegram from New Zealand which had arrived late afternoon on 21st June, the day they had brought Erika home.

"It's sad news," Dieter said, taking Jeannie in his arms. He waited while Jeannie read the telegram. Dad had died on 21st June and the funeral had been held three days later. They cried on each other's shoulders. It had been expected but they could not believe it.

"I thought we could visit with little Erika at Christmas but it's too late. He's gone to his rest," Dieter said through his tears.

"I can't believe Dad's gone. It just doesn't seem real," Jean sobbed.

Dad had appeared almost his usual self when they visited two months earlier. Letters that had come from home did not portray the depths of his suffering and rapid decline. Jean wrote a letter to Mum saddened that Dad had gone. She went on to tell Mum about her first grandchild.

"Erika looks very much like the photo you have of me at about six weeks old, lying on a crocheted rug looking cross-eyed. She is feeding well and putting on weight. I just wish you could be here!"

Mum wrote back and enclosed the photo Jean had described. As Jean opened the letter and showed the photo to Dieter their first thought was, where did Mum get that photo of Erika? They had not had any developed yet! Then the penny dropped, it was the photo of Jean. Mum told them that as soon as she had got the news about Erika she had gone straight to Dad's bedside. Even though he was in a coma by then she took his hand and spoke gently in his ear. 'We have a beautiful little granddaughter called Erika. Jean and the baby are both well.' She didn't expect any response but she was sure he understood. 'He squeezed my hand. Maybe that was what he had been waiting for. Then he slipped away.' The father that Jean had loved and Dieter had longed for all his life!

CHAPTER FORTY-EIGHT

On a Friday late in August 1971 Dieter was musing as he looked out the door at the store. It was almost closing time and he was looking forward to the weekend. There was not a cloud in the sky. Sun streamed in across the floorboards towards the counter making the two naked light bulbs above it seem ineffective. A dark figure entered through the light, blocking it out for a moment, a European whom Dieter had never seen before.

"Hello. I am Ted Barnett," the stranger said holding out his hand.

"Dieter Klier," he responded, shaking the proffered hand. "Pleased to meet you."

"I'm new in this area. Just been appointed as business advisory officer for the district."

"Oh I see. So what does that entail?"

"The government is eager to encourage the indigenous people to form their own companies with support from people like me. Obviously it won't happen overnight – there's a lot of groundwork to do," explained Ted.

Dieter nodded, but he did not understand why Ted had visited him.

"I would like to talk with you sometime," Ted went on, looking around at those in the store. The smell of smoke from their cooking fires pervaded the place. It clung to their clothes and hair. Customers were pointing and talking as they chose their goods. One took out a wad of leaves from his bark belt, unwrapping it to reveal shilling pieces to pay for his wares. The store boys waited patiently while the transaction took place.

"Why don't you come to my place in the weekend," Ted suggested. "We can talk over coffee."
"That sounds good," said Dieter.
"Do you have family?"
"Yes, my wife Jeannie and a new baby six weeks old."
"Why don't you bring them too! We have two young children and my wife Min doesn't get out much."
"Sounds fine to me."
So it was settled. Dieter felt a stirring of excitement as he shut up shop and went home to talk to Jeannie.
"Why do you think he took the trouble to visit me?" Dieter asked.
"I guess he's getting to know people. Anyway it would be impossible to phone you," she said with a laugh.
"Maybe he is going to offer me a job," continued Dieter. "I don't feel secure with Mantons now – have not even seen the plans. We moved to Mendi on the proviso that this expansion was happening but I don't think it will."
"Well, let's wait and see if Ted has got anything to offer on Sunday. We can make up our minds then."

On Sunday afternoon the little family turned up at the address provided by Ted. Jean carried Erika in her arms, dressed in a smocked frock, while Dieter brought the baby basket. Ted and Min welcomed them at the door and introduced themselves as their two young children peeped shyly from behind them. After the preliminary small talk and oohs and aahs over the baby Min made coffee and brought out the biscuits while Ted and Dieter began to talk business. Min and Jean spoke about their children and the vagaries of life in New Guinea. Occasionally Jeannie heard snippets from the men's conversation but she would need to connect the dots later. Dieter was talking about his work for Namasu in Lae and Chimbu, as well as Waso in Kandep. As he recounted challenges he had experienced with Waso, Ted realised that Dieter had developed skills in nurturing business development and offered him a job.
"Think about it, talk it over with Jean and get back to me," Jean heard Ted say. So Dieter had been right. She knew he took his responsibility for her and the baby seriously. Maybe this was the answer he was seeking.

As soon as they were in the truck Dieter spilled the beans.
"Well there's a job waiting for me if we want it."

"Where is it?" Jean asked.
"It's just behind that range." Dieter pointed to the mountains. "Still in the Southern Highlands at a place called Nipa."
"So what would you be doing there?"
"Managing a native owned company. I would be the only European working for them, apart from Ted in a supervisory role."
"That sounds good."
"I think so. Nothing is happening with Manton brothers and I don't believe it ever will. If he was serious we would have seen some action by now. I don't want another repeat of Waso."
On Monday Dieter contacted Ted to tell him he would take the job with Nipa Sura. They sat down and talked about the position and conditions of pay as well as accommodation.
"I am afraid the house at Nipa is unfinished – just a shell with external doors only, internal partitions and gaps in the floor. It is not lined inside and there is no water supply or toilet. The accommodation has been used for camping only! You'll need temporary accommodation but I'll arrange that for you. There is a carpenter on the station and he should be able to assist you," Ted explained.
"Well it won't be the first time I've done a bit of building," Dieter replied. "I am sure we'll manage."

Darrel admitted he was relieved when Dieter handed in his resignation as things had changed in Mendi. An existing trading company there had already begun to build a new commercial outlet and Mantons were reluctant to invest more money in the place in the near future. So Jean and Dieter moved to Nipa by plane in September 1971 when Erika was three months old. There was no road connecting them to Mendi but the weather was warmer with the altitude 1000 feet lower. Ted had found temporary accommodation for them in a government house that was empty until the new assistant district commissioner arrived. A single man named Rex was living there too –an agricultural officer.

The Nipa Sura complex was a large wooden building with a trade store across the front facing the road. The store needed more shelves and a large counter, which were completed first to get trading established. Behind the trade store was an office containing a safe and a desk with a two way radio on it for communication with the outside world. Dieter used this to order trade store supplies and building materials. The house itself was in the rear of the building, sunny, airy and spacious. A four wheel drive landcruiser would enable Dieter to take supplies to the trade stores in outlying areas – Poroma and Margarima.

Dieter's days were full with running the store, supervising building projects, ordering materials and putting as much time as possible into completing their home. It was often difficult for him to resist the urge to drive himself harder to get the project finished soon but there were elements of it that were beyond his control. Sometimes Erika's charms won out. One Sunday afternoon after a pleasant lunch Jeannie persuaded him to spend some time with them. While Jean made coffee, Dieter relaxed on the bed playing with Erika. As Dieter rolled over onto his back and began to toss Erika into the air Jeannie came in.

"Be careful," she warned, "I've just finished feeding her."

"She'll be all right," Dieter insisted as he carried on. Two minutes later a call for help, "Jeannie," alerted her to the fact that she was right. Shaking her head as she walked in with a hand towel, Jeannie threw it to him to mop up his chest. Erika was all right, but Daddy wasn't.

"Have you looked at her feet?" Jean asked him.

"What's special about them?" Dieter wanted to know.

"They are just like yours. I noticed it yesterday. Her big toes are shorter than the second toes."

Dieter looked at them and picked each little foot up in turn and kissed them. "My beautiful daughter!" he said.

CHAPTER FORTY-NINE

Five weeks later Rex announced that the ADC and his family were arriving in seven days so they would all have to vacate their residence. "What will we do?" asked Dieter. "I haven't even got all the supplies yet for the house, let alone finished it."
"There is another house you could use. It was the original home of the first patrol officer. A grass house with kunai roof, pitpit walls and a separate house-cook. But you wouldn't want to stay there too long," he said.
After inspecting it Dieter said, "it's not ideal but it's a roof over our heads. I'll really be under pressure to get our own place finished."
    It did not take long to unpack and settle in. All they needed to do was make the bed and unpack enough kitchen utensils to be able to make a meal. After all it should not take too long to finish their abode they believed. Tanks collected rain water off the roof of the house-cook and this was piped to the kitchen tap. Inside, the floor was made of rough sawn timber with a wood stove for cooking and heating water.
    While Dieter worked feverishly on the house in the cool evenings after dinner, Jean sat in the kitchen knitting, reading or writing letters. Erika slept in her basket under the table to shade her from the light of the kerosene lamp overhead. A cat that had been given to them dozed in front of the stove. Minnie kept watch beside Jean. It was warm and cosy but others thought so too. After about half an hour as the night drew in around the house-cook, black noses and beady eyes peeped through the pitpit matting. Gradually they

became braver and ventured out, rat bodies and tails on dainty feet, looking for stray morsels of food. Jean carried on her evening's occupation waiting for Cat to pounce. Rats scuttled in panic and hopefully Cat's speed would be rewarded with a savoury supper. Minnie too would join in but there was only one problem with this method of pest control. Both Minnie and Cat had a limited capacity and there was a limitless supply of Rat! Once Minnie and Cat were outside munching and crunching Jean's role came in to play. Beside her on the floor was a pile of magazines. As the rats returned to the floor, brazen as ever, she threw a magazine into the arena and they darted back into the walls for a time. So Jean's evening continued, baby snuffling in her basket under the table, Cat and Dog now snoring, magazines skittering across the floor at her command, rats scattering or squeaking.

At the other end of the village Dieter worked on. There were no rats or anyone else to hear him dragging sheets of plywood across the rough floor and hammering them into place, then sanding them ready for several coats of polyurethane. But that was just the floor. He still needed to line and paint the walls. Then there was the problem of getting water to the house. He hoped the tank would arrive soon.

In his early life Dieter had learned to live with scarcity, especially of food and later when he lived with his mother there was the lack of love. Now his life had changed – there weren't enough hours in the day to get the job done and supplies were difficult to come by and slow to arrive. His love for Jeannie and Erika drove him on. For Jean she experienced scarcity of time with Dieter but she understood his dilemma and supported him with tasty meals and love. Erika enjoyed her life, oblivious to much of what was going on around her. She had the love and care of both parents, food on tap and protection from anything that could harm her. In the day time she slept outside under a tree in her pram with Minnie keeping guard beside her until she finished her nap. At night she slept in her basket hung on the woven matting wall right beside her parent's bed.

At last Dieter had finished lining the house, painting the walls and three coats of polyurethane had been applied to the floor. There had been three attempts to obtain a water tank and Dieter hoped he would be successful this time. The first tank was despatched by road to Mendi. Unfortunately the truck had rolled off the road and the tank was crushed to a useless heap. Tank number two arrived safely at the bulk store in Mendi, waiting to be flown in to Nipa, when the bulk store caught fire and the solder melted leaving the metal warped and twisted.

"I have organised for the next tank to be flown directly from Hagen to Nipa," Dieter said to Jean. "Surely nothing else can go wrong. We only need one."

After six weeks of living in the rat infested house it was imperative that they move out as soon as possible. Jean suggested they do it straight away.

"But there's still no tank, no guttering to catch rain and no toilet," Dieter stated.

"I know but the place is lined, the windows and fly wire are in place to keep the insects out. Above all, there are no rats!"

Dieter was not convinced. He was deep in thought when Jean added, "Look there are sheets of corrugated iron lying round the house. Why can't we set them up in a row directly below the eaves so that the rainwater can run down the iron sheets into a 44 gallon drum. Then you've got fresh water!"

"But we'll need a toilet!"

"Yes. How long would it take to dig a hole and knock up a shelter around it?" Jean wasn't going to be put off. "I can cook on the primus, we can bath in the big tub and sleep in our beds. It will be much safer for Erika."

"All right. I get your point. I will get Oivi to build the toilet frame tomorrow. We've got pitpit matting all ready and iron for the roof."

The next day the family moved in. Admittedly Jean had to wait for the toilet to be built complete with a box seat before she could relieve herself. Insects liked to congregate on the surface of the water supply but that could soon be rectified. Jean skimmed them off the surface before collecting drinking water and then boiled it. A spare internal door was set up on trestles in the living area for Jeannie to cook one pot meals in the pressure cooker on the primus. Bathing was done in a large galvanised wash tub in the middle of the floor. The same tub was used for washing the clothes outside next to the improvised hot water service Dieter had made – a 44 gallon drum cut in half and placed end on end with a fire burning under the lower half that had a cut away section for stoking it. The top was filled with water. Thank goodness Erika was still breast fed and not mobile.

FLIGHT TO FREEDOM

That evening after dinner as Erika slept in her cot Dieter and Jeannie lay back propped up on pillows on the bed, the kerosene lamp shedding light on the scene.

"Well it's a relief to have moved in," Dieter began, "but did you think it would be like this when you married me?"

"No and I bet you didn't either. But we have got everything we need. What more could we want?"

"Well a water tank for starters and a plumber to install it, kitchen cupboards finished so that we can put things away, easy chairs to sit on rather than the bed! Do you want me to continue?"

"Oh you are an old grump. I think you need a few early nights!" Jeannie laughed.

CHAPTER FIFTY

At last Jeannie felt she could settle in to life in Nipa. Their house was warmer in the evenings even though they had no wood stove. It was a bright open house with views of the rainforest sloping away from their windows. At night the companionable hiss from the kerosene lamp brightened their small world. Jeannie bathed Erika in the evenings so that Dieter could enjoy conversation with his daughter, endearments, cooing and cuddles from him rewarded with smiles and baby words in reply. As Dieter dried and dressed her for bed Jeannie pumped the primus and lit the methylated spirits. A ring of blue flame danced around the centre of the primus, heating the pipes so that when she released the kerosene under pressure it ignited easily.

While the family waited for the 'extras' to complete their home Dieter pushed forward with building a bulk store. He needed a dry rat-proof space where he could store rice, cabin bread, biscuits and clothing or blankets as well as cartons of tinned mackerel and MaLing duck. The concrete floor helped somewhat. Oivi was the carpenter, while his sister Winnie worked in the store. They were from the coast and had come to Nipa with the family as their father had work there as a policeman. In the afternoons when a rain storm hissed along the valley dropping its contents as it went, Oivi worked on building kitchen cupboards. Co-dependency developed as Dieter's workers Winnie, Oivi, Sule and Marame appreciated being employed full time and Dieter and Jeannie valued the fact that they were hard-working and honest. Kumian, the house boy, was a boon to Jeannie, carting water, heating it and doing the washing by hand. Friendship with the local member of Parliament Tegi Ebial also developed. It was important for economic development in the area that Nipa Sura should be successful. Erika always responded to his bright smiling face until the day he turned up in native costume, his face transformed with sing sing paint. In spite of talking to her in his soft mellow voice and saying her name she screamed at him and hid her face.

After months of waiting the water tank finally arrived by Pilatus Porter direct from Hagen, intact, perfect, standing tall. Jeannie could not wait for the plumber to come from Mendi to install it. She was like a child at Christmas. It was a momentous occasion when rainwater from the tank was piped to the taps in the house.

"Everything is happening now. But I'm still glad we moved in when we did," Jeannie commented.

"Yes so am I. It's good having the bulk store finished too. I'm not falling over cartons in the store, but I think I'll need a cat in the bulk store to keep down the rats," Dieter replied.

"Just one? What if it gets stolen and eaten?"

"Well a pregnant female would be good. That way I should have a constant supply."

CHAPTER FIFTY-ONE

It was mid November, heading into the wet season. The mornings were noticeably warmer. The sun streamed in the windows.
"Bravo Sierra, Bravo Sierra! November Zulu calling."
The radio in the office, their only contact with the outside world apart from planes, crackled into life.
"November Zulu, Bravo Sierra," Dieter responded.
"Hi Dieter. It's Lex here. Just wondered if you'd like visitors for Christmas. Over."
"Yes that would be great. The whole family? Over."
"Only eight of us," Lex chuckled. "We plan to travel by truck. Over."
"You are mad! What route will you take?"
"From Kandep to Margarima, then on to Nipa. I was talking to a kiap and he said we should do it in a day. As long as we take some spare logs. They do it all the time."
"Knowing you, you'll find a way!" Dieter said. "See you for Christmas then."
Lex laughed, "Okay, see you then. Call you later. Over and out."
" Bye, over and out."

Jean was delighted when Dieter told her. "There's only one problem though. Where will they all sleep?"
"I've had a think about that. You will need space to use as a school room when you're teaching young David next year. If we built a two-roomed guest house out the back, it could serve as a school room as well."
"That'd be great."

"I still want to get the hot water service in too," he continued. "That would make it easier with two babies in the house."

Work started immediately. Bush timbers (round poles) were harvested for the frame. Woven matting was made for the walls, two layers with kunai grass in between as insulation and for the thatched roof as well. The door was made of pit sawn timber from the Catholic mission mill and two small louvre windows were procured from the local government council. Woven matting served as a floor covering. In no time at all it was up and habitable, just two rooms, a table and two home-made single beds.

The masterpiece however was the hot water service for the main house. Once the rainwater tank was installed the plumber connected a pipe to a smaller tank on the roof. A hand pump was used by Kumian to fill the tank which supplied cold water to the taps in the house. Now this was to be used to feed a 44 gallon drum surrounded in concrete and set on its side on rocks near the large tank. Gravity fed this tank and the water was heated by a fire lit underneath it. Another pipe soldered into the top bung-hole carried hot water to the kitchen and bathroom. Each afternoon it was Kumian's job to light a fire under the drum to ensure there would be hot water for quick showers and washing dishes. With well practised economy and the concrete insulation round the drum the water was still lukewarm for washing dishes after breakfast the next day. It was a marvellous system. That evening after a hard day's work Dieter soaked in the bath tub.

"Ah, this is the life," he said, proud of his achievement with the help of the plumber. "Mirry and Lex will think they are staying in a five star hotel."

"Especially if they have a bath in the evening under the stars!"

CHAPTER FIFTY-TWO

Early in January the family had just finished breakfast. Erika sat in the high chair, banging a spoon on the tray saying "ba – ba – ba." Sun was streaming in the living room windows. The rattle of breakfast dishes being washed by Kumian could be heard and another swish of the sunlight soap shaker in the water. He paused with his hands in the water and turned his head to talk to Jean.

"Scuse mi Missus. Mi laik go long ples bilong mi," he said.

"Aren't you happy here." Jean hoped she was not going to lose him. She knew it must be difficult for him away from home, living among a tribe that spoke a different language.

"Yes Missus, mi happy. Mi laik lukim meri," he said with a shy smile.

"Ah, that is good. I will tell masta."

Dieter, like Jean, did not have a problem with Kumian taking time off. They knew that it must have been very lonely for him when he finished work for the day and went to his accommodation where he could speak only pidgin to those who had learned it. Dieter arranged for Kumian to fly on a back load to Mendi. From there he could get a ride on a truck to the Ialibu turnoff. The rest of the journey would be by foot.

It could be some time before Kumian came back. A wife was not to be bought at face value, there had to be negotiations back and forth between the two families until both sides were satisfied with the deal. Kumian would need to borrow the agreed bride price from his clan. This debt would be repaid when other men in his clan wanted to buy a wife or two! Only after the wheeling and dealing had occurred would the wedding ceremony take place, followed by a feast of pigs cooked in an earth oven or umu.

"You will need your own house when you come back," Dieter suggested to Kumian. "I will get Oivi to build it over there behind our house."

"Thank you masta," Kumian beamed. "I will come back quickly – if I can."

CHAPTER FIFTY-THREE

Shouts came from the yard at Nipa Sura. It was mid morning and a fine day so far. Dieter hoped it would stay that way until the job was done. It was the dry season with balmy weather heading for 30°C today so they should be lucky. Across the road from the store a Pilatus Porter revved its engines preparing for takeoff after disgorging its load – a 4KVA diesel generator and drums of fuel. Ted had said it would happen when there were enough funds in the general account and there it was! Dieter had been given the dimensions over the radio so a concrete pad was custom made, ready and waiting. The boys called to each other, shouting encouragement as they inched the generator on tree trunk rollers closer to its destination. The land sloped away from the house to the bottom of the yard where the pad was situated.

Dieter called out instructions as he supervised. "Isi, isi!"………. "Holim!"……… "Holim pas!"………… "Pasim, pasim!" He didn't want the heavy generator to careen down the hill off the rollers. Sweat glistened on scantily clad bodies but at last the generator had arrived safely. Now the task was to use the rollers to lever the generator onto the bolts that had been set in the concrete. Dieter breathed a sigh of relief when the generator finally sat in place, looking as if it had always been there.

Then Oivi set the rollers into the ground around the pad to support the roof. A row of power poles led from the generator back up to the house. Two holes were bored in each of these poles, the one at the top to take the power line to the house, the lower one for a wire cable attached to the generator's governor that terminated in the bedroom on Dieter's side of the bed. It came up through the floor and was firmly secured to a bolt. Dieter did not want to run to the bottom of the yard at night in his pyjamas to turn the lights out!

It was wonderful to have electric lights at the flick of a switch. They were much better to read by in the evening, without the smell of kerosene hovering overhead. When the day was done and they sank into bed all Dieter needed to do was reach out and yank on the bolt and hold it up in order to turn the lights off. At first he tended to release it too soon. The generator would pause as if thinking about it and then chug back to life with all lights blazing.

"I'll soon get the hang of it," he said. "At least it will build up my muscles."

CHAPTER FIFTY-FOUR

With the advent of power and a freezer it became possible to stock fresh meat and fish brought in from the coast. This would be for sale in the trade store and among the European station personnel. The generator was going from 4 pm to 10 pm each day, this being sufficient to keep the goods frozen.

One night some time after the generator was turned off Dieter and Jean were woken to strange noises outside the back door. That end of the house was about four feet off the ground and as yet no steps had been built. It was a cold night with only a sliver of moon as Dieter got out of bed to investigate. What was it? He could hear snuffling and snorting and the sound of heavy feet on the gravel path. He unlocked and opened the back door, shining the torch around. A black something was resting its nose on the doorstep. As Dieter turned the torch light on it, red eyes reflecting the light stared back at him. He was terrified. As he became accustomed to the dim light he noticed a mythical beast, a voodoo bull. Its breath was vaporising in the night air and arrows at odd angles were sticking out of its rump. He slammed and locked the door returning to the bedroom.

"What is it?" Jeannie asked.
"A bull!" he replied.
"Are you sure?"
"You go and look then."
"Well what do we do? It might fall into the excavations for the septic tank. Then we wouldn't get any sleep."

So Dieter got a bath towel, opened the door and waved it furiously at the bull. Then he slammed the door and got back into bed.
"It must be Tegi's bull. That's the only bull around here."
"Yes I'll talk to him in the morning."
It turned out on investigation the next day that the bull had done the rounds of the government compound where the native workers lived. A policeman's uniform shorts, shirts and socks hanging on the clothesline had been mangled and chewed. Hence the arrows sticking out of its behind as they tried to move it along.
"Tegi's done everything he can to keep it fenced," Dieter explained. "Now the bull will be slaughtered and the meat sold to pay compensation. He's asked if he can keep it in the freezer."
"Get a nice piece for us," Jean suggested, "and I'll make you some sauerbraten. It might be a bit tough otherwise!"
On another night the generator had been silenced as Dieter and Jean settled down to sleep. Darkness enveloped them and soon Dieter's heavy breathing indicated he was already asleep. It had been a busy day for Jean, making bread, (no bakery down the road if you wanted fresh bread), doing the ironing with a kerosene iron, looking after a mobile Erika almost a year old now, as well as cooking meals. She gave a satisfied sigh as she began to succumb to the peace and quiet of the night. What was that? A scratching, clicking sound came to her ears.
"Where's the torch?" Jean gave Dieter a prod. She did not want to get out and walk around the bed to get it in case she stood on something.
"What's wrong? I was asleep," Dieter complained.
"There's something clicking near my head."
Dieter searched under the pillow and over the back of the bed on the floor.
"There's nothing there," he replied. "Are you sure it's not in your head?"
"Like you and the bull!"
"Go to sleep. You'll be right." Dieter rolled over.
As soon as he turned off the torch and Jean put her head on the pillow it started again.
"There is something there. I can hear it," Jean announced, turning on the torch again. This time Jean took matters in her own hands. She knew she wasn't dreaming. After a second cursory sweep with the

torch light under the pillow and near the head of the bed she began to peel off the pillow case. Snuggled in the corner was the culprit, a black shiny rhinoceros beetle about two inches long, waving its pincers angrily at them.

"So there you go. I wasn't imagining it," Jean stated.

"No my Darling. I'll take it outside to find somewhere else to sleep," Dieter replied, always the gallant gentleman.

CHAPTER FIFTY-FIVE

It was unbelievable that Erika was one year old already. Mind you so much had happened in the intervening months since her birth, Jean reflected. They had moved four times if she began with the upstairs flat in Mendi. The proud mother looked at Erika in her highchair eating a snack. She was healthy and strong, beginning to pull herself up on furniture. Soon she would be walking. She fed herself somewhat messily but above all she was a happy child, speaking a few words and making up others in her own language. She was good company!

Erika and David, the ADC's son that Jean was tutoring, had their birthdays on the same day. David was turning six. So Jean and David's mum Anna had decided to have a combined birthday party. At two o'clock when Erika woke from her afternoon sleep Jeannie dressed her in the outfit she had made on the hand powered sewing machine - rompers that buttoned on the shoulders with a pinafore over the top. She had managed to get a pale green and white pinstriped material in Hagen. The pinafore was edged with green ric-rac. Wearing new white shoes and socks she looked a picture. The proud parents had had fun choosing a wibbly wobbly toy and a book for her as well – Go Dog, Go! Of course she needed a birthday cake. Jean made one in a round loaf tin and another from the same mixture in a square pan. The round one was iced and then more icing dribbled down it to look like a fat candle. Jean put a red jube on top shaped like a flame.

In the corner of the living room were a dolls' pram and a baby that Dieter's mother Oma had sent. Erika loved it. She could walk along with it until she became too excited, leant on the handle and crashed. She would soon get the hang of it! An assortment of books and toys had come from Jean's family in New Zealand. Grandma had sent a dress, dolls clothes and bedding for the doll's pram. All this from family Erika had never met.

Jean pressed a cellotaped bow onto Erika's hair, Dieter put the high chair and doll's pram onto the truck and they were ready to go. It was a beautiful sunny day and Anna had set everything up outside on the lawn. David hopped about excitedly but Erika was her usual happy self, not yet aware what the fuss was about. David played with the small number of friends available on the station and Erika played with her new toys while the adults chatted and laughed. Soon there was lolly water, sandwiches, savouries, biscuits, cakes and coffee for the adults. The candles were lit (but the lights could not be dimmed) and happy birthday was sung. It was a happy occasion. That evening after dinner the proud parents lit another birthday candle on the leftover cake, sang happy birthday once more and tried to teach Erika to blow out the candle. But that would have to wait till next year.

Erika soon learned the trick of wheeling her dolls pram in a straight line without the 'up and down, hit the ground' motion. She loaded Minnie's puppies into it and they added weight and stability. From time to time she needed to stop and poke a wayward tail or foot back into the pram. Then came the day when Dieter took Erika out to the bulk store to show her the kittens. Afterwards she told her Mum excitedly, "pussie's got puppies." The kittens never got a ride in her pram because they were born and bred for the sole purpose of keeping the rat population under control.

It had not been confirmed yet but Jean was sure she was pregnant again. She was experiencing the same symptoms as last time but it was early days yet. They were both excited at the prospect. The day was dull, overcast but not cold or raining. Erika was toddling around playing happily after breakfast, the smell of porridge still lingering in the air. Kumian was rattling dishes in the sink as he cleaned up. Jean had planned to tidy out the cupboards in the living room where Erika often helped herself to things and then stuffed them back before someone came and caught her at it. But that would have to wait.

FLIGHT TO FREEDOM

Earlier she had found a spot of blood in her knickers and that was a concern. Dieter had gone to see Jan, the mission sister at Tiliba to see what she advised. Jean waited. Would she need to fly out to Hagen? How long would she be away? She tried to relax on the bed and put these anxious thoughts from her mind.

"Mino, Kumian, mino," Erika said. She knew that he made good milo for her and Kumian was always glad to oblige. Jean smiled to herself. She was thankful that they had such a reliable house boy, one they could trust. She heard the crunching of tyres on the gravel drive outside the bedroom window as Dieter drove in.

"Sometimes that happens, Jan said. It may be nothing to worry about but she says you should have a week's bed rest," Dieter stated.

"That's a bit of a nuisance, but I guess I have to do as I am told."

"Yes. Jan suggested I take Erika to her place each day and bring her back after tea. She can play with her children and you can have a proper rest."

"That is kind of her."

"It you need anything to read just ask her," Dieter added.

So Jean spent the week resting, reading and knitting. Kumian cooked the meals and Jean was relieved that she had taught him to prepare some basic recipes. Dieter fetched Erika home each evening, fed her and bathed her, gave her a bedtime story and tucked her in for the night. There had been very little spotting and Jean was reassured. It looked as though it was a false alarm.

Two days later it started again. Erika had spent the day with Jan. Dieter popped his head round the door.

"I'm off to pick up Erika. You okay?" he asked.

"Yes I am fine."

Dieter gave her a peck on the cheek. "Won't be long."

It seemed that he was no sooner out of the drive when the pains started. The store was shut for the night and Kumian was not in the house. Jean went to the back door and called loudly as she held her stomach. It was no use. He could not hear her. There was no response. She headed back to bed but then thought she should go to the toilet on the way – their new inside toilet, thank goodness. The pains were getting worse as she relieved herself, when suddenly with a whoosh something else came away. Jean stood up and stared into the bloodied toilet bowl. There was nothing to do but flush the toilet and get back into bed.

When Dieter came back he was horrified, anxious and felt guilty for not being there.

"You had better get Jan," Jeannie said.

In a flash Dieter was gone again, taking Erika with him as he went to tell Jan that Jeannie had miscarried.

After checking Jeannie out to make sure she was all right Jan said, "it can be nature's way of getting rid of something that's not perfect. Maybe it wasn't well attached and wouldn't be nourished as it should. I am sorry. I suggest you go to Hagen for a checkup on Monday just to make sure everything is fine. If you need me in the weekend, let me know."

"Are you sure she is all right?" Dieter asked.

"Yes, the pains are easing and there's not excessive bleeding. It's sad that it happened but it's probably for the best. You've got a beautiful little girl so there is no reason why you can't have another baby later."

It was an anxious weekend as all Dieter's fears returned. What if Jeannie started bleeding badly? He would not be able to get a plane in if the weather was bad or it was night time. A missionary had died after giving birth in Kandep, away from the hospital. Jeannie tried to reassure him that she was all right. At last it was Monday and he was able to get Jean on a plane. He radioed Barbara to pick them up and take them to the hospital. Erika stayed at Nipa with Jan Jones. The verdict in Hagen was that she would need to have a D and C that day and would have to overnight in Hagen. All went well, a general anaesthetic followed by the procedure, then discharged from hospital four hours later. Dieter took Jeannie's arm and supported her as they walked out. She felt quite woozy from the anaesthetic. Barbara turned on a lovely meal and Jeannie was soon ready for bed.

The next morning Dieter did some business in town and then they headed for the airport. They were booked to fly out that afternoon with Scotty when he returned from another job. By the time Scotty, an ex crop duster, turned up the weather was closing in.

"It's no good to the north of Giluwe," an incoming pilot said, "but it's still okay to the south."

Their little plane, a Cessna 185, was packed to the gunnels and when they were airborne Scotty circled three times to get enough altitude to make it over the gap. Jean and Dieter sat in the rear of the plane having crawled in through the small door above the wheel that bounced them up and down along the tarmac when the plane took off and landed. Storm clouds were gathering as they flew to the north of Giluwe, not to the south. As the weather intensified the plane battled on, the wind flicking up the nose of the plane and the stall warning sounding at frequent intervals. Dieter and Jean were holding hands in the back of the plane praying for dear life. What if they didn't make it back? What would happen to Erika? The awful realisation hit them that they had been very remiss. No one in Nipa had any idea of their family contact details. There was an address book that they may be able to ferret out but that would not be much use. No one knew Jean's nee name and Dieter's mother had remarried before she left Germany. There was nothing they could do except pray harder. It was a long flight. The trip that usually took just under an hour, took one and a half hours but it seemed longer. Scotty conceded that it was not good weather for flying and he should stay overnight.

Next morning Scotty refuelled the plane with avgas and took off in brilliant sunshine. Jean and Dieter left the contact details for both sides of the family in the office and made sure that people knew it was there. Some weeks later they discovered a bottle of Drambuie hidden in a cupboard. It must have been a gift from Scotty, who liked a drop himself

CHAPTER FIFTY-SIX

Six weeks later in November 1972 they had planned to go to Wewak on holiday. At the same time Dieter hoped to make fresh business contacts for Nipa Sura. However he was concerned. Jeannie was still not well after the miscarriage. He suggested it might be better for her to stay home and rest.

"No," she said emphatically. "There is a hospital in Wewak if I need it, more than I have here. And you need a holiday too. We haven't had a holiday since our honeymoon. You never stop. Your bouts of malaria are becoming more frequent. A holiday will benefit all of us."

"All right," Dieter admitted. "I guess that's true."

Jean was relieved. With each bout of malaria Dieter needed to be hospitalised. His body rejected the standard anti-malarial tablets, rushing them out his rear end before they had a chance to work. Each time Jean needed to organise a plane to fly in with cargo and backload Dieter, shivering and shaking violently with fever, to Mount Hagen hospital. After two to three days on the drip he would be restored to health and able to come home again until next time. Jeannie strongly believed that a holiday might work wonders for Dieter's health.

So there they were, in the plane on their way to Wewak. The smell of aircraft fuel lingered in the cabin. Bright sunshine reflected off the clouds beneath giving them a white phosphorescent glow as the propellers whirled and the engine droned on. Cradling Erika in her arms, Jean dreamed of being at the beach once again, taking Erika there and letting her dabble her toes in the sea, evoking squeals of delight. She had never stayed in a hotel before. It would be wonderful – no housework to do, quick easy meals of tropical fruits while they were out and about, then an evening meal in the hotel restaurant.

The plane started to descend as they neared Wewak.
"Nearly there!" The pilot turned to Jean with a cheerful smile. "Are you all right?"
"No! I have terrible pain behind my eyes." Jean's reverie had been rudely interrupted by it. She had no idea what it was.
"Sorry, I'll take the plane down more gradually," he said as he pushed forward on the joystick decreasing the angle of descent. Almost immediately Jean noticed a lessening in the pain.
"I've never had that happen before," Jean said.
"Maybe a bit of sinus," he suggested.
"But I've been well, no hint of sinus at all."
Once on the ground they stowed their luggage in the boot of the small rental car and with a map from the agency set off for the hotel. The air was hot and humid – sticky Jean called it.
"No worries," Dieter said as he turned on the air con in the car but nothing happened. "It's buggered! Wind your window down and we'll get a cool breeze."
"That's true, but only while we're driving," Jean replied.
Brilliant red poinsettias stood in a row outside the hotel as they turned into the entrance and stopped by the main door. In a matter of minutes the car was unloaded and in the below-ground car park, while the family and their luggage were escorted to their room, island music accompanying them through the corridors.

It was shaded and cool in their room with an air con that worked. She drew back the drapes and looked down onto a central courtyard with frangipanis in bloom.
"Look," Jean commented, "my wedding flowers. We've come to the right place."
It was late in the day so they decided to have dinner before going to the beach. The light was fading as they donned their swimming togs and headed for the beach. Memories of Lae flooded Dieter's mind while Jean thought of the beach at home in New Zealand. The sea here would be much warmer.
"We are going to the beach," they told Erika who at seventeen months did not seem to mind one way or the other.

"She hasn't a clue what a beach is," Jean said.
"Yes but she will soon. She'll love it."
But she didn't! Holding her parents hands as they walked down the beach with Erika between them she began to pull back. Jean picked her up.
"It's all right, Honey," she said as they walked closer to where the waves ran up the beach. Dieter took her from her mother's arms and bent down to let her feel the warm water on her feet as another wave rushed up to swallow her. Erika screamed and drew her feet up.
"No, no," she pleaded.
"What's wrong sweetie? It's the sea! Just water like your bath. You love your bath," coaxed Daddy.
But the damage was done! Erika did not like the beach or the sea. Even in daylight! Dieter and Jean asked themselves what the problem had been. Was it the sound of the waves crashing and rolling in at night? Or the water on the wet sand threatening to wash it from under her? Maybe just fear of the unknown. They tried to cajole her, building sandcastles, digging holes or dabbling in a bucket of water. Nothing they did could change her mind. Every time they went to the beach one or other of her parents had to hold her or she would scream. Jean was having severe sinus problems too and could not stand the oppressive humidity. For the rest of the week they made a few forays to the beach. Otherwise Jean did a little shopping for clothes for the family and stayed in the cool air in the hotel with Erika. Dieter kept appointments with businessmen in the town and struck bargains. As the week proceeded Dieter had trade store goods delivered to the airport where they were kept in open sheds with sides of arc mesh and a wide overhanging iron roof on top, ready for their return flight.
"It's been a good time away from Nipa," Jean told Dieter as they were packing up to return home. "I feel much better."
"I do too. More relaxed. I am pleased you persuaded me to come."
"But it'll be good for me to have a checkup in Goroka. Just make sure everything is okay."
"Yes definitely." Dieter wanted to be sure things were back to normal.
When they arrived at the airport the boys had just finished loading the cargo under the pilot's supervision. Finally it was all fastened down in the plane under a heavy duty rope net.

FLIGHT TO FREEDOM

"Dieter, you sit up the front beside me," the pilot said. "I'm afraid you and the baby will have to sit in the rear."
"No worries," Jean smiled. "I am used to it."
"Had a good holiday?" he asked.
"Yes but the time has flown."
"In you pop then."
Dieter held Erika as Jean crawled headfirst into the rear seat with a bag of pineapples and pawpaws and buckled herself in. Then he passed Erika through to Jean.
"There you are, sweetie. All safe and secure."
Jean watched as the men took up their positions in the cockpit. There was enough space above the cargo to see them but she could not hear their voices as the pilot started the engines and they taxied out.

Erika looked out the window as they circled over the ocean before heading north.
"Ook, Mama, aw gone."
"Yes love, all gone. Bye bye, sea."
Erika waved happily, chattering on as she looked at a book with Jean. She was speaking well for her age, her proud mother thought, not that there was another tot of her age to compare. Jean settled back with her head on the head rest, breathing in the smell of tropical fruit at her feet. It was rare that they could buy a pineapple in Nipa and never pawpaw. They were taking some of Wewak back with them. Little did she know that there was more than fruit near her feet.

There were few clouds today as they approached Goroka. Below, the United Nations hospital sprawled close to the airport waiting to welcome them.
"I'll stay with the plane," Dennis said as he sat in the doorway unwrapping his lunch. "No hurry! See you when you are done."
It was dim and cool in the hospital after the plane. Following the signs to the outpatient department they soon found the reception desk.
"My wife needs a checkup after a miscarriage. She was treated at Mt Hagen immediately afterwards," Dieter explained, "but it's taken a long time for the bleeding to stop."
"I'll put you on the list. Please take a seat," the receptionist said with a smile.
"We've got a plane waiting for us at the airport. On our way home to the Southern Highlands. It won't be too long will it?"

"No I will put you on top of the list."

"Thanks."

A variety of people walked past, staff with sandals on their feet, clipping along, others with wide splayed bare feet brushing the floor. A smell of disinfectant wafted out as doors opened and closed again. Voices could be heard behind curtains. Soon a gynaecologist appeared.

"This way please." He ushered them to a room. "Now how can I help you?"

Jean told them about the miscarriage and subsequent events. "We just want to know everything is all right," she said looking over at Dieter with Erika on his knee.

"Right then. Hop up on the bed and I'll examine you."

After poking, writing and peering he pronounced his verdict. "You are fit and well again, fine to go ahead with another pregnancy if you wish."

"Thank you," Dieter said before Jean could get a word in.

"That's good to hear," she said.

So back to the plane they went and were soon up in the air again heading for Nipa. Jean gave Erika a sandwich and drink from her cup and soon she was asleep. It was a pleasant flight. Jean was pleased to see home as the plane circled the compound and came in to land from the south. Although Erika had had food and a short nap on the plane it would be good to give her a run around before an early dinner and into bed.

Winnie, Sule, Oivi, Marame and Kumiane lined the strip as Dennis opened the door and the family alighted. They moved forward, ready to help unload and carry the store supplies to the bulk store. Dieter thanked Dennis for the flight and gave the workers their instructions before heading down the road with Jeannie and Erika. He was hanging out for a coffee. They were almost home when there was a hullabaloo back at the plane. Everyone was fleeing, shouting, running helter-skelter away from the cargo when suddenly they turned around as one and headed back. Dieter shrugged as he continued home with the suitcase and let Jeannie into the house. She pointed Erika in the direction of her toys and ride-on motorbike before filling the kettle and putting it on the stove. Taking the fruit from the bag she arranged it in a bowl on the table and stood back to admire it.

Just then there was a knock on the door. As Jean poured the coffee Dieter went to see who it was.

"Come and have a look at this," he called.

"Aaah!" Jeannie recoiled in horror.

Sule stood there with his prize, a dead snake, its head held firmly in a forked stick.

"Where did that come from?" she asked.

"In the plane, near the rear door. It's not poisonous," Dieter added.

"But I wouldn't have known that. It's the first snake I have ever seen. We don't have them in New Zealand!"

Later that evening when Erika was snug in her own bed Dieter and Jean agreed that it had been wonderful to have a break, a change of scenery.

"I was able to relax and swim again," Dieter said.

"I enjoyed the beach too," Jean added, "and the tropical fruit and fresh fish."

Dieter chuckled about the snake. "It must have crawled into the open shed at the airport and gone to sleep."

"If it had poked its head out in mid-flight you and Dennis wouldn't have been able to help. I would have been terrified. Tried to get out in midair I reckon."

"Well, we all need some excitement, don't we?"

Erika was not the only one to be initiated into the Wewak experience.

CHAPTER FIFTY-SEVEN

Christmas was approaching. Government personnel at Nipa and in the surrounding district had young children so they decided to put on a Christmas party for them and any others who would like to attend. A party with Santa and all the trimmings at Margarima. An overcast day did not spoil the outing. Jean packed a picnic lunch of egg sandwiches with home-made bread. There was high excitement in the clearing that the subdued light could not dim. Adults talked amongst themselves as they set out the picnic food.

"Keep a lookout for Santa," the children were told as they ran around excitedly.

"Will he have something for us?"

"Does he know where we are?"

The mothers answered questions again then continued talking. Erika was eighteen months old so she was not bothered about the fuss – yet!

Finally the children heralded Santa's arrival. A well rounded Santa (also known as Mike) complete with cotton wool beard, appeared on the back of a landcruiser, ho-ho-ho-ing and ringing a bell. He apologised for not having a sleigh with reindeer. He was seated in a bucket chair trying to placate two goats who were tied to it. When the truck stopped the goats were keen to get going! As soon as he had tied up his 'reindeer' Santa produced a large sack of gifts. Excitement mounted.

"Stand in a line, like good boys and girls," Santa said as he sat on his chair and patted his knee for the first child. Jean, holding Erika in her arms, waited at the back of the queue while the older children jumped around. What a good idea, Jean thought. To provide a visit from Santa for children who lived in such isolated places. Next it was Erika's turn. As Jean and Erika approached Mike reached out with his gloved hand to pat her little head. Terrified, Erika turned her head away and sunk her teeth into Mummy's shoulder, making her eyes smart. No one realised the pain that had been inflicted until Jean handed Erika to Dieter and rubbed her shoulder. Santa gave Erika's gift to Jeannie.

"I'm sorry," he said. "I've never had that effect on a young lady before."

CHAPTER FIFTY-EIGHT

As Dieter drove around the district supervising workers in outlying trade stores he sometimes met missionary nurses holding maternal and child welfare clinics. On one such occasion he had been alerted to the fact that people who were unconscious and could not communicate were considered to be dead. Often the clan placed the person on a stretcher and left them in a burial cave. If they regained consciousness, the cold, lack of food and water and the fear of witchcraft associated with death would rapidly bring about their demise. If Dieter became aware of any burial caves on his travels the nurse suggested he should check them on the way past and take any living person back on the truck to the nearest mission station for medical care.

One day Dieter was told that a young lad about twelve years old had been deposited in a burial cave on the side of a hill to die. Dieter found that the boy was still alive so took him in the truck to the Catholic Mission at Poroma where the nuns cared for him. He went out to Hagen hospital as a medical emergency.

Mid morning on New Year's Day 1973 Dieter heard a feigned cough outside the back door. Native houses did not have a door so a cough was how they alerted others to their presence. Dieter opened the door and saw three lepers standing there. The government doctor boy who usually drove to the outlying villages with their medication had not visited since before Christmas. Please could he help them? There was no one around on the government station. Dieter was very moved by their plight. It was the first time he had seen lepers.

FLIGHT TO FREEDOM

Although he had no tablets Dieter took out gentian violet and painted it on the sores – on hands, faces and toes. He was unsure whether it would help but they went away happy, feeling that someone cared.

Mid afternoon on the same day Bev, a nurse from the Uniting Mission, arrived. A young woman was lying in the back of the jeep covered with a blanket. She had been brought on a litter from the village, in labour but unable to give birth. Tribal customs made it taboo for men to touch a woman who was menstruating or in labour. Gradually this belief was being eroded by European influence but there was still reluctance for some.

"Please would you radio Hagen for a medical emergency flight," Bev requested.

"I can try," Dieter replied, "but the battery on the radio is flat and being New Year's Day there is unlikely to be anyone on the other end." Dieter lifted the blanket and looked at the patient. She was slight, hardly more than a child, barely moving, just tensing and moaning as the pains came.

"I'll do my best," he said turning on the radio. It crackled into life as he called the airport. To his immense surprise and relief, Heli, the chief pilot, answered them. Yes he could fly in! He had just popped in to pick something up when he heard the radio.

Later Bev reported that both mother and baby were alive and well but the father of the child, who had remained in the village, disowned it. Everyone knew that it was impossible for the baby to survive. Therefore it must have been replaced with another man's child.

CHAPTER FIFTY-NINE

On Sunday mornings the family was able to sleep in. The store was not open and Kumian had a day off. Erika was playing happily in her cot while Mum and Dad had a quiet cup of coffee in bed.
"Time for breakfast," Jean said. She padded bare foot into the living room to open the curtains. Thin slivers of sunshine peeped around the closed curtains but it was cool inside, cooler than usual. Thinking nothing of it she drew the curtain aside.
"Dieter," she called in shock, "what's happened?" Disbelief coloured her voice as Dieter jumped out of bed to investigate. Everything, absolutely all the vegetation had turned black overnight.
"It's frost! Must be frost."
"But we don't get frost in New Guinea," Jean stated.
"It looks as though it is."
And Dieter was right. Although there was no oral history or any living memory of this phenomenon, frost had hit hard, making the landscape look like a burnt out war zone. A smell of rotting vegetation pervaded the air outside. The grass was black, all the gardens were black, the trees too. Everything! In one foul swoop!
"How will the people get on?" Jean asked Dieter. "Kaukau is their staple diet. Without that they will starve."
"It's a fluke of nature. Should be all right. Just leaf damage."
But there was more to come. Frost hit hard three nights in a row and the implications dawned. Everything was annihilated. Nothing was frost hardy. Not sweet potato, grass, bamboos, or pandanus palms which provided a crop of nuts (protein) every second year only. Not

to mention their wealth – a man relied on pigs to buy a wife or two. What would the pigs eat? The Australian government declared a state of emergency in the affected areas of the highlands. Rice and tinned mackerel were flown by hercules aircraft from Hagen to Mendi where caribou planes took over to transport the goods to Nipa, the caribou being able to land and take off on shorter airstrips. Sweet potato tubers were also supplied for replanting, to kick start the new crop.

Dieter assisted with the distribution, transporting food to outlying villages. He worked long hours, driven by his memories of hunger as a child. Poor sleep patterns developed from the stress and his health began to suffer.

"The people are not used to the diet, you know," Dieter told Jeannie. "Many of them are getting diarrhoea now."

"Poor things! It'll be good when everything is back to normal."

Little did they realise that the frost would be followed by drought, requiring water to be flown in.

CHAPTER SIXTY

There were two things Jean was learning about her husband. He liked order and beauty. One Saturday in March they were finishing their lunch.
"I am going to clean up along the side of the house near the tank. That bush is taking over so I'll trim it back."
"Good oh. I'll do some baby knitting while Erika has a sleep," replied Jean.
Dieter had already built a swimming pool. He had been given bags of cement when the rain had driven into the shed at the airstrip. The local council officer was throwing them out. Dieter had been wondering what to do about the spring up above their place that oozed water into the yard. Problem solved. Put in a pool with water on tap. He had landscaped around the pool, put a carved wooden statue on one end and planted coffee trees on the slope below. There was a small vegetable patch there too, in front of the generator shed. The water in the pool was cold. Jean thought it would warm up with the sun on it, but it never seemed to happen. She had one or two swims in it. Erika was not keen on it at all but Daddy was! He would often have a dip in the pool at night. Said it helped him to sleep. He would come back to bed freezing cold and expect Jeannie to warm him up.

Today he needed to catch up on some gardening. Grabbing a bucket, spade and secateurs, Dieter headed for the garden. The bush that he had planted by the tank had large leaves and long white pendulous trumpet shaped flowers with a beautiful perfume. Dieter pruned the bush, taking cuttings from it as he went. Standing back, he checked the shape of the bush to see that it was uniform. Then he dug a garden along the side of the house to plant out the cuttings. The weatherboards on the house had been protected against the elements with creosote, creating a black background to set off the green bushes and the white flowers.

"Like a coffee?" Jean asked some time later.

"Always," Dieter replied. "Come and see what I have done."

Jean was impressed. "It'll be beautiful when they grow and the perfume floats into the house."

"Yes, they don't take long. I'll look out for more plants from the bush that I can propagate to fill in the spaces."

"That'll be good," Jean said not realising the danger to Erika from the angel trumpet bush.

Sunday morning Dieter woke up with the little finger on his right hand red and swollen. As the day wore on the throbbing and swelling increased. Jean gave him paracetamol every four hours and bathed the finger in salt water. In spite of these ministrations the finger turned black and Dieter developed a fever. Thank goodness it was Monday tomorrow. He would need to go out to the hospital again. So next morning they followed the usual procedure – Dieter went as a back load by plane to Hagen, Jean stayed home to look after the store. Dieter was given intravenous antibiotics and his finger was getting better he said. By Thursday he was fed up with hospital and missing his family. He wanted to go home. The doctor agreed and prescribed him two more weeks on antibiotics.

"How's your finger?" Jean asked when he arrived home. Dieter showed her. It was red and wrinkly now that the swelling was going down, with scaly skin peeling off.

"Is it sore?" she asked him.

"No not at all!"

Eight days later on 7th April things were not good. Dieter was still taking his antibiotics but woke up on Friday feeling weak and unwell. To get to the toilet he asked Jeannie for help, holding her arm and using door frames and cupboards for support as well.

"How is your finger?" Jeannie asked. "Let me see."

"It's not sore," Dieter replied.

"It looks no better than last week," she said.

CHAPTER SIXTY-ONE

All was not well. Maybe there was something more sinister brewing and it was Friday. No time to wait and see. Jean helped Dieter into the office to call on the radio and get everything organised – store goods from Hagen to Nipa, then Dieter to backload to Goroka hospital this time, where there were better facilities and more staff. Anxiously Jean watched the weather and waited, her ears straining to hear the aircraft arriving. At last! By this time Dieter was finding it difficult to sit up. The pilot was shocked as he watched Dieter and Jeannie walk over the road to the airstrip. He was always so energetic and enthusiastic. In view of the situation he decided it would be best to remove seats and lay Dieter on the floor of the plane, strapping him down for safety. As the emergency flight took off Jean turned with a heavy heart, praying that all would go well.

"Goodbye Daddy," she said to Erika, but Erika buried her head in Mummy's shoulder as she repeated the words in a small voice.

Back at the house workers and customers from the store had congregated near the steps, squatting or sitting cross-legged on the ground. Jean was not prepared for the wailing that started. The ritual loud weeping that went on for days after someone died. They sent shivers down her spine. Is that what they expected? Taking Winnie aside she asked her to try and move the people on. Dieter was not dead and should be back in a few days. With a sigh of relief she watched Winnie coax them away from the back door and quiet descended on the house. There was nothing Jean could do but wait. She made herself a cup of tea and settled down with Erika on her lap to read her a story. Kumian had made a large pot full of vegetable soup for lunch. It would do for dinner as well with some toast, while they waited for word from Dieter over the radio. It would probably be after five before tests had been done and a diagnosis obtained. Jean proceeded through the afternoon like an automaton doing what she had to do, trying not to worry about Dieter. At least he was in the hospital now where he could get the help he needed. She made afternoon tea for Erika, then left her to play while she folded washing and put it away in the drawers. A bath, then into her pyjamas, followed by dinner and bed.

With relief Jean heard their call sign come over the radio. It was Dieter – so he wasn't any worse, thank God. She hurried through and responded. Dieter was angry!
"Stupid doctor! Doesn't know what she is doing. Took a blood test knowing that I was still on antibiotics and nothing has shown up. Said I am having a breakdown and need to go south."
Jean was stunned, then her logical brain kicked in. "All we need is a medical certificate to get pro rata leave pay and our airfare south. We've been here just four months short of your contract so that's good. We don't have to believe what she says!"
At last Dieter calmed down. "Okay," he said.
"Where do you want to go?" his wife asked.
"New Zealand," he said without a second thought. "The Southern Alps remind me of Germany and you should be near your mother when the baby is born."
"I'll scrounge packing crates from anyone who will give them to me and start packing."
"You will have to contact Ted to come in and work out the leave pay and look at the books," Dieter added.
"All right, I'll do that. You're best to stay there at the hospital and when everything is settled we'll meet you in Goroka on our way home. You call me on Sunday for an update." Jean did not want the worry of having him home again till there was a resolution of the problem.

CHAPTER SIXTY-TWO

So Jean set to work. She was three months pregnant and only just on her feet again, having suffered from acute lethargy in the first months as she had with Erika. She called on the radio scheds and soon had boxes and crates stacked in the lounge. Now she could start packing. Jan Jones offered to look after Erika during the day to leave Jean free to get the job done as quickly as possible. The only items of furniture they had were a carved Chinese writing desk with a chair and a camphorwood box. Jean packed the baby clothes in there for their next child. Then she packed three suitcases of clothes to take with them, being mindful that autumn in Dunedin would be very cold in comparison to Nipa. They would need the pushchair with them on the plane. By Saturday evening when Dieter radioed Jean had finished packing the kitchen, bathroom and bedrooms.
"Just the lounge to do," she said proud of her effort.
"That's great but are you all right. I worry about you."
"I am fine. Erika is worried about you. She has developed diarrhoea so I've put her back in nappies. She cries for you in her sleep too."
"The poor little thing. Give her a kiss and a hug from Daddy."
"I'll do that. She's been sleeping in bed with me so that I can comfort her without getting out of bed all the time."
"You look after yourself," said Dieter.
"I will. How are you?"
"No different. Just the same. When do you think you'll get here?"

"I'll finish the packing tomorrow. Ted's coming on Monday. Not sure how long that will take. Then I have to settle accounts in Hagen, go to the bank to transfer funds, see to getting our cargo down to Lae and shipped home. I think it'll be Tuesday afternoon at the earliest," replied Jean.

"I love you. I miss you both. Sorry to do this to you," Dieter said as he signed off.

"Love you too. Bye."

By Sunday evening everything was packed and ready to go. Jan and Russell had asked them to stay with them for Sunday and Monday nights. Jean made sure that she was back at Nipa Sura each evening to waylay Dieter's fears and worries. Everything went smoothly with Ted - checking the books, doing a stock take and arranging for airfares and pro rata leave pay. It was a tedious job but had to be completed before Jean and Erika could leave. Around 4 pm on Monday Ted said his farewell, giving Jean an envelope and letter of thanks for Dieter. A plane was organised for first thing Tuesday to take Jean and Erika to Hagen. They were on their way.

Bright and early on Tuesday morning their plane arrived. Jean and Erika said a last goodbye to Minnie and Prince (one of Minnie's puppies). Russell had said he would find good homes for them.

"If you can't," Jean said, close to tears, "I don't want to hear about it. Please put them down."

"I'll do my best," he reassured.

All of their cargo was still in the house and would be moved to the shed on the airstrip that day ready for back loading to Hagen and storage there that Jean would arrange at Hagen airport. Erika perked up as they stowed their suitcases in the plane and buckled themselves in.

"See Daddy," she said.

CHAPTER SIXTY-THREE

Jean didn't know what she felt – sad at leaving, relieved to be getting Dieter home for medical treatment, tired after all the packing, excited about seeing her family again only Dad would not be there. That still seemed unreal. She looked down on the Nipa Sura compound and waved once again in case any of their faithful staff were watching.

In Hagen Jean talked to Heli regarding their cargo. It could not be insured until it reached the wharf in Lae, he explained, because of the 'raskals' that preyed on trucks going down the Highlands Highway, leaping from embankments onto the back, slashing through tarpaulins and hiffing cargo over the side to be picked up by the rest of the gang. They would just have to take that chance, Jean decided. There was no other way to do it.

With Erika in the pushchair Jean visited the bank and arranged their finances. She booked tickets to Goroka for that afternoon. Dieter had done the bookings in Goroka from there to New Zealand but there was one small problem. He did not have a cheque book with him so he could not uplift them till Jeannie arrived. After accounts were paid at Burns Philp and the chemist there was one last thing Jean needed to do. She bought Erika a little suitcase of her own to hold her books, toys and colouring materials for the long trip ahead of her. Once these were neatly packed it was time to get some lunch and head back to the airport.

They arrived in Goroka at 5p.m. that evening. Dieter still looked very tired and felt weak but he had discharged himself from the hospital and booked in to a guest house for the overnight stay.

FLIGHT TO FREEDOM

"We'll have to pay for the air tickets first thing in the morning. They'll be closed now," Dieter told Jeannie.

"Yes and send a telegram to Mum too." Jean's mother had no idea that they would be in New Zealand to stay in a couple of days. Dieter had booked the travel in Goroka but did not have an itinerary. Jean had refrained from sending a telegram until she knew the time of arrival. As Dieter gave Erika a goodnight kiss and cuddle that evening she snuggled in and said "my Daddy." All was well in Erika's world.

Bright and early on Wednesday morning they were up, breakfasted and at the travel agents to pick up the tickets. Next down to the post office. The telegram said:

Arriving Christchurch New Zealand 3 pm Thursday 13th April. Will contact about arrival time in Dunedin. Love Jean, Dieter, Erika.

"I wonder what she will say," Dieter asked.

"She'll be so excited!"

Another telegram went to their friends in Sydney asking if they could stay overnight. If they were not at the airport then they would know it was not convenient and so stay in the People's Palace instead. With a sense of relief at last they sank into their seats on the plane, heading for Port Moresby for a stopover then on to Sydney. Dieter felt bad. He was unable to carry the suitcases or even help with Erika.

"I am sorry," he said. "You shouldn't be lifting suitcases."

Jeannie took his hand. "It's all right. I am fine. We are on our way now so you can get the medical treatment you need. That's all that matters."

"But I don't want you to lose this baby too."

"I know. But I'm over three months now and feeling well again. Just like with Erika."

Dieter smiled and laid his head on her shoulder. "I don't know what's wrong with me."

Erika chatted away as they flew south. She was good at that, had talked copious amounts of baby talk from an early age and now was speaking in intelligible sentences at twenty-two months old. She was a happy child and entertained herself well. Once they arrived in Moresby they had to wait for a connecting flight. After a drink and a snack Mummy helped Erika open the case and choose something to occupy herself. She chose her favourite book 'Go Dog Go!' Opening the book she turned the pages one by one reciting the words from memory. Other passengers waiting in seats opposite looked on in amazement. Here was a baby (she was dainty and slim, having just lost weight after a bad bout of measles) reading a book aloud. "Dog" turn page, "big dog, little dog" turn page, look from left to right "black dog, white dog," and so it went on. Her speech was so clear. It was truly an amazing performance, all from memory, but the onlookers were not to know that. Her proud parents did not enlighten them.

Dieter was concerned as they waited in Port Moresby. He had been in consultation over the past months with the Prime Minister Michael Somare and a delegation from Germany regarding trade and finance. During the meeting he had been privy to highly confidential information. His fears overtook him as he waited. In spite of the humidity he shivered. What if Michael Somare had heard he was leaving the country? Would he demand a debriefing session or worse still, not allow him to leave until the deal was finalised. Jeannie tried to calm his fears but knew that it was futile until they were safely in the air again. At least Erika was entertaining the passers-by with her storytelling. They looked like an ordinary family going home on leave, apart from the extraordinary baby who could read before she was out of nappies!

All went to plan in Sydney and they were able to stay with their friends. After a night's rest, back to Sydney airport, then heading for Christchurch. With a sense of relief Dieter and Jean took in the beauty of the mountains as they crossed from the west and approached Christchurch airport. They had talked to Erika about going to see Grandma, someone whom Erika had never met and obviously had never related grandma to her photo. She loved to write 'etters' to Grandma when her Mum wrote a letter. But that did not prepare her for meeting Grandma and knowing who she was, what she looked like. As the plane descended into Christchurch Erika looked down onto paddocks on the Canterbury Plains. She pointed excitedly, "Look Mummy, there is Grandma."

"No darling, that's a cow." There were huge gaps appearing in Erika's knowledge of the big wide world.

FLIGHT TO FREEDOM

ABOUT THE AUTHOR

Jean Klier was born in New Zealand where she lived for the first twenty years of her life. After training as a primary teacher she left New Zealand to teach in the Western Highlands of Papua New Guinea where she met and married Dieter. Travels to other places followed and they are now retired and living in Albury, New South Wales, Australia with an adorable but nutty dog Peanut. Their three adult children and four grand children are scattered around Australia and New Zealand.

Flight to Freedom is Jean's third novel in the series **The Heart Still Sings** following on from **The Alien Nation**.

If you enjoyed reading **Flight to Freedom** you may want to read what happened next. See over for a preview of the final book in the series – **Family Echoes**.

Family Echoes

CHAPTER ONE

Once through customs Dieter asked at the desk for a flight to Dunedin that day but there were none. He was exhausted and keen to finish travelling and see a doctor. He was not feeling any better.
"There is the Starliner," the attendant said. "It leaves from the bus depot at 7 pm and arrives in Dunedin at midnight."
"Yes we'll do that," Dieter replied.
Jeannie looked doubtful at first. Then she said, "I suppose that would be all right. We could have tea beforehand and Erika will sleep all the way."

A quick ring to family friends in Christchurch who picked them up, fed them and deposited them back at the bus station. They would contact the Dunedin family and tell them the arrival time. This was the last part of their arduous journey. Erika sat on Jean's knee looking out the window as the bus wound its way through the outskirts of Christchurch. Erika saw her first real sheep and horses and more cows. Soon street lights came on and much to the amusement of other passengers she tried to blow out the candles. Where had this child come from? Soon the entertaining chatter came to an end and Erika slept.

The journey was uneventful with Dieter and Jeannie snatching sleep where they could. The bus stopped at towns along the way, disgorging some passengers and welcoming others. Jeannie watched as they drove into Oamaru, past her grandparents' old home in Thames Highway. Memories flooded in of sitting on Grandad's knee, snowy white, curly-haired Grandad with a moustache, while he sang songs to her in his wobbly voice. She had lived in Oamaru for six months as a baby when her mother was ill. Auntie Vera and Uncle Ivan (her Dad's brother) who had no children of their own, looked after her, spoilt her but then had to give her back when her Mum recovered. It must have been a difficult thing to do, Jean thought as they called into the bus depot to drop off mail bags and a passenger. Jean could not believe her eyes. There on the platform stood Auntie Vera, Uncle Ivan and Auntie Edna. Was she dreaming? No! Jean and

Dieter clambered off the bus, waking Erika in the process. There were kisses and hugs until Uncle Ivan saw Erika.

"My baby," he said, gently taking her from Jean. Erika was having none of it. She screamed loudly and lunged for her mother. "Sorry," he apologised. "I didn't think. She looks so much like you when you stayed with us."

"That's all right," Jean consoled him.

Uncle Ivan was usually quiet and undemonstrative. Erika's likeness to her mother had caught him off guard.

Next stop was Dunedin. Jean's Mum and sister Ann were waiting for them, wrapped up in thick coats and scarves. Mum cried tears of joy as they hugged each other. It had been two years since she'd seen them and Dad had died just two months later.

"Let's get your luggage into the car," said Ann. "You'll be staying with us for a couple of nights until we can find you other accommodation. We are living in a holiday batch at Doctors Point so it's pretty small but we'll fit in."

"I am staying the night too," Mum added. "There's no room at all at my flat."

In the car to Ann and Keith's place Jean outlined Dieter's health problem to Ann, a nurse.

"I'll take you to accident and emergency at the hospital tomorrow morning. Better not muck around."

CHAPTER TWO

In the morning while breakfast was being prepared Grandma decided to take Erika for a walk in the sunshine. There had been a frost overnight but it promised to be a sunny day. Taking Erika's hand Grandma walked along the path in her wobbly way. She had one leg much shorter than the other. Soon Erika slipped her hand out of Grandma's and walked over the dewy grass, sliding her feet over the silver dampness.

"Come and walk on the path dear," Grandma coaxed. "You will get your shoes all wet."

She nearly fell over when Erika replied, "not right at this moment!" Erika and Grandma were getting to know each other.......

FLIGHT TO FREEDOM

JEAN KLIER

FLIGHT TO FREEDOM

www.ingramcontent.com/pod-product-compliance
Lightning Source LLC
Chambersburg PA
CBHW060506090426
42735CB00011B/2129